1 MONTH OF FREE READING

at
www.ForgottenBooks.com

By purchasing this book you are eligible for one month membership to ForgottenBooks.com, giving you unlimited access to our entire collection of over 1,000,000 titles via our web site and mobile apps.

To claim your free month visit:
www.forgottenbooks.com/free1303942

* Offer is valid for 45 days from date of purchase. Terms and conditions apply.

ISBN 978-0-428-69783-9
PIBN 11303942

This book is a reproduction of an important historical work. Forgotten Books uses state-of-the-art technology to digitally reconstruct the work, preserving the original format whilst repairing imperfections present in the aged copy. In rare cases, an imperfection in the original, such as a blemish or missing page, may be replicated in our edition. We do, however, repair the vast majority of imperfections successfully; any imperfections that remain are intentionally left to preserve the state of such historical works.

Forgotten Books is a registered trademark of FB &c Ltd.
Copyright © 2018 FB &c Ltd.
FB &c Ltd, Dalton House, 60 Windsor Avenue, London, SW19 2RR.
Company number 08720141. Registered in England and Wales.

For support please visit www.forgottenbooks.com

1999 Illinois Register

Rules of Governmental Agencies

Volume 23, Issue 10 — March 05, 1999

Pages 2,735 – 2,823

published by
Jesse White
Secretary of State

Index Department
Administrative Code Div.
111 East Monroe Street
Springfield, IL 62756
(217) 782-7017
http://www.sos.state.il.us

Printed on recycled paper

TABLE OF CONTENTS

March 5, 1999 Volume 23, Issue 10

PROPOSED RULES

CENTRAL MANAGEMENT SERVICES, DEPARTMENT OF
  Standard Procurement
    44 Ill. Adm. Code 1 2735
NUCLEAR SAFETY, DEPARTMENT OF
  Freedom Of Information Procedures
    2 Ill. Adm. Code 1076. 2737

ADOPTED RULES

HIGHER EDUCATION, BOARD OF
  State Matching Grant Program
    23 Ill. Adm. Code 1038 2747
POLLUTION CONTROL BOARD
  Primary Drinking Water Standards
    35 Ill. Adm. Code 611. 2756
  Standards For New Solid Waste Landfills
    35 Ill. Adm. Code 811. 2794

EMERGENCY RULES

CENTRAL MANAGEMENT SERVICES, DEPARTMENT OF
  Standard Procurement
    44 Ill. Adm. Code 1 2812

NOTICE OF PUBLIC HEARINGS

NATURAL RESOURCES, DEPARTMENT OF
  White-Tailed Deer Hunting By Use Of Bow And Arrow
    17 Ill. Adm. Code 670 2819

JOINT COMMITTEE ON ADMINISTRATIVE RULES-
STATEMENT OF OBJECTIONS, SUSPENSIONS, RECOMMENDATIONS,
PROHIBITED FILINGS & APPROVALS

ELECTIONS, STATE BOARD OF
  Established Political Party And Independent Candidate Nominating
  Petitions
    26 Ill. Adm. Code 201, Filing Prohibition 2820
  New Political Party Nominating Petitions
    26 Ill. Adm. Code 202, Filing Prohibition 2821

i

PUBLIC HEALTH, DEPARTMENT OF
    Asbestos Abatement for Public and Private Schools and Commercial and
    Public Buildings
        77 Ill. Adm.Code 855, Objection 2822

JOINT COMMITTEE ON ADMINISTRATIVE RULES

    Second Notices Received 2823

ISSUES INDEX I-1

Editor's Note: The Cumulative Index and Sections Affected Index will be printed on a quarterly basis. The printing schedule for the quarterly and annual indexes are as follows:

    April   16, 1999 - Issue 16: Through March   31, 1999
    July   16, 1999 - Issue 29: Through June   30, 1999
    October 15, 1999 - Issue 42: Through September 30, 1999
    January 14, 2000 - Issue 3: Through December 31, 1999 (Annual)

INTRODUCTION

The **Illinois Register** is the official state document for publishing public notice of rulemaking activity initiated by State governmental agencies. The table of contents is arranged categorically by rulemaking activity and alphabetically by agency within each category. The Register also contains a Cumulative Index listing alphabetically by agency the Parts (sets of rules) on which rulemaking activity has occurred in the current Register volume year and a Sections Affected Index listing by Title each Section (including supplementary material) of a Part on which rulemaking activity has occurred in the current volume year. Both indices are action coded and are designed to aid the public in monitoring rules.

Rulemaking activity consists of proposed or adopted new rules; amendments to or repealers of existing rules; and rules promulgated by emergency or peremptory action, Executive Orders and Proclamations issued by the Governor; notices of public information required by State statute; and activities (meeting agendas, Statements of Objection or Recommendation, etc.) of the Joint Committee on Administrative Rules (JCAR), a legislative oversight committee which monitors the rulemaking activities of State agencies; is also published in the Register.

The Register is a weekly update to the **Illinois Administrative Code** (a compilation of the rules adopted by State agencies). The most recent edition of the Code along with the Register comprise the most current accounting of State agencies' rules.

The Illinois Register is the property of the State of Illinois, granted by the authority of the Illinois Administrative Procedure Act [5 ILCS 100/1-1 et seq.].

REGISTER PUBLICATION SCHEDULE 1999

Issue #	Copy Due by 4:30 p.m.	Publication Date	Issue #	Copy Due by 4:30 p.m.	Publication Date
Issue 1	Dec 21, 1998	Jan 4, 1999 *	Issue 28	June 28	July 9
Issue 2	Dec 28	January 8 **	Issue 29	July 6 ***	July 16
Issue 3	January 4, 1999	January 15	Issue 30	July 12	July 23
Issue 4	January 11	January 22	Issue 31	July 19	July 30
Issue 5	January 19	January 29	Issue 32	Jly 26	August 6
Issue 6	January 25	February 5	Issue 33	August 2	August 13
Issue 7	Feb 1	February 16	Issue 34	August 9	August 20
Issue 8	February 8	February 19 ***	Issue 35	August 16	August 27
Issue 9	Feb 16 ****	February 26	Issue 36	August 23	September 3
Issue 10	February 22	Mar 5	Issue 37	August 30	September 10
Issue 11	March 1	Mar 12	Issue 38	Sept 7 **	September 17
Issue 12	Mar 8	Mar 19	Issue 39	Sept 13	Sept 24
Issue 13	March 15	Mar 26	Issue 40	September 20	Oct 1
Issue 14	March 22	Apr 2	Issue 41	September 27	Oct 8
Issue 15	Mar 29	Apr 9	Issue 42	Oct 4	Oct 15
Issue 16	Apr 5	Apr 16	Issue 43	Oct 12 ***	Oct 22
Issue 17	Apr 12	Apr 23	Issue 44	Oct 18	Oct 29
Issue 18	Apr 19	April 30	Issue 45	Oct 25	November 5
Issue 19	April 26	May 7	Issue 46	November 1	November 12
Issue 20	May 3	May 14	Issue 47	November 8	November 19
Issue 21	May 10	May 21	Issue 48	November 15	November 29 *
Issue 22	May 17	May 28	Issue 49	November 22	Dec 3
Issue 23	May 24	June 4	Issue 50	November 29	Dec 10
Issue 24	June 1 **	June 11	Issue 51	Dec 6	Dec 17
Issue 25	Jun 7	June 18	Issue 52	Dec 13	Dec 24
Issue 26	June 14	June 25	Issue 1	Dec 20	Dec 31
Issue 27	Jun 21	July 2		Dec 27	January 7, 2000

* Monday following a state holiday.
** Tuesday following a state holiday.
*** Since the state holiday is a Monday, the deadline is Noon on Tuesday.

Printed by authority of the State of Illinois
March 1999 - 600 - GA-964

DEPARTMENT OF CENTRAL MANAGEMENT SERVICES

NOTICE OF PROPOSED AMENDMENTS

1) Heading of the Part: Standard Procurement

2) Code Citation: 44 Ill Adm. Code 1

3) Section Number: Proposed Action:
   1.2020   Amend

4) Statutory Authority: 30 ILCS 500

5) A Complete Description of the Subjects and Issues Involved: Raises the
   small purchase threshold from $10,000 to $25,000 per year solely for
   concession contracts at the Illinois State Fairgrounds in Springfield and
   DuQuoin when such concessions offer or display exhibits, goods, or
   services to the general public. The threshold will be raised through the
   normal rulemaking process for all other purposes.

6) Will this rulemaking replace any emergency rulemaking currently in effect?
   Yes

7) Does this rulemaking contain an automatic repeal date? No

8) Does this rulemaking contain incorporations by reference? No

9) Are there any other proposed rulemakings pending on this Part? No

10) Statement of Statewide Policy Objectives: Rulemaking does not affect
    units of local government.

11) Time, Place and Manner in which interested persons may comment on this
    proposed rulemaking: Interested persons may submit written comments
    within 45 days of the date of publication to:

            Stephen W. Selple
            720 Stratton Office Building
            Springfield IL 62706
            217/782-9669

12) Initial Regulatory Flexibility Analysis:

    A) Types of small businesses, small municipalities and not for profit
       corporations affected: None

    B) Reporting, bookkeeping or other procedures required for compliance:
       None

    C) Types of professional skills necessary for compliance: None

13) Regulatory Agenda on which this rulemaking was summarized: This rule was

DEPARTMENT OF CENTRAL MANAGEMENT SERVICES

NOTICE OF PROPOSED AMENDMENTS

not included on either of the 2 most recent agendas because: The need for
the rulemaking did not come to the Department's attention until after the
timeframe in which a regulatory agenda was to be filed.

The full text of the Proposed Amendments is identical to the text of the
Emergency Amendments that appear on page ___ of this edition of the Illinois
Register.

DEPARTMENT OF NUCLEAR SAFETY

NOTICE OF PROPOSED AMENDMENTS

1) Heading of the Part: Freedom of Information Procedures

2) Code Citation: 2 Ill. Adm. Code 1076

3) Section Number: Proposed Action:
   1076.10   Amendment
   1076.20   Amendment
   1076.100   Amendment
   1076.110   Amendment
   1076.200   Amendment
   1076.210   Amendment
   1076.300   Amendment
   1076.310   Amendment
   1076.400   Amendment
   1076.410   Amendment
   1076.Appendix B Repeal

4) Statutory Authority: Implementing and authorized by the Freedom of Information Act [5 ILCS 140] and Section 5-15 of the Illinois Administrative Procedure Act [5 ILCS 100/5-15].

5) A Complete Description of the Subjects and Issues Involved: The fees the Department charges for reproduction of public records have not been adjusted since their revision in 1989. Departmental staff has done research into the fees charged by other State agencies and the costs of some of our related activities in providing information to the general public. From this research, it became apparent that the Department has been undercharging its FOIA requestors by a significant amount. By modifying this rule, the Department will be able to provide a more efficient program by encouraging the use of electronic formats (for example, by providing certain mailing lists by electronic copy or paper copy in lieu of pre-printed adhesive-backed address labels that had been available in the past upon request); reduce staff time in the duplication and production of records; and generate additional revenues to cover the Department's cost of providing information. This amendment will also clarify the Department's document inspection procedures; update citations to the Illinois Compiled Statutes (ILCS) and make editorial changes to conform to JCAR format.

6) Will these proposed amendments replace emergency rules currently in effect? No

7) Does this rulemaking contain an automatic repeal date? No

8) Do these proposed amendments contain incorporations by reference? No

9) Are there any other proposed amendments pending on this Part? No

10) Statement of Statewide Policy Objectives: The requirements imposed by the proposed rulemaking are not expected to require local governments to establish, expand, or modify their activities in such a way as to necessitate additional expenditures from local revenues.

11) Time, Place and Manner in which interested persons may comment on this proposed rulemaking: Comments on this proposed rulemaking may be submitted in writing for a period of 45 days following publication of this notice. The Department will consider fully all written comments on this proposed rulemaking submitted during the 45 day comment period. Comments should be submitted to:

    Rose Miller
    Freedom of Information Officer
    Department of Nuclear Safety
    1035 Outer Park Drive
    Springfield, Illinois 62704
    (217) 785-9860 (voice)
    (217) 782-6133 (TDD)

12) Initial Regulatory Flexibility Analysis:

   A) Types of small businesses, small municipalities or not for profit corporations affected: The Department does not believe that this amendment will impact small businesses, small municipalities or not for profit corporations.

   B) Reporting, bookkeeping or other procedures required for compliance: None

   C) Types of professional skills necessary for compliance: None

13) Regulatory Agenda on which this rulemaking was summarized: January 1999

The full text of the Proposed Amendments begins on the next page:

ILLINOIS REGISTER 2739

DEPARTMENT OF NUCLEAR SAFETY

NOTICE OF PROPOSED AMENDMENTS

TITLE 2: GOVERNMENT ORGANIZATION
SUBTITLE D: CODE DEPARTMENTS
CHAPTER XVI: DEPARTMENT OF NUCLEAR SAFETY

PART 1076
FREEDOM OF INFORMATION PROCEDURES

SUBPART A: INTRODUCTION

Section
1076.10   Summary and Purpose
1076.20   Definitions

SUBPART B: PROCEDURES FOR REQUESTING PUBLIC RECORDS

Section
1076.100   Person To Whom Requests Are Submitted
1076.110   Form and Content of Requests

SUBPART C: PROCEDURES FOR DEPARTMENT RESPONSE
TO REQUESTS FOR PUBLIC RECORDS

Section
1076.200   Timeline for Department Response
1076.210   Types of Department Responses

SUBPART D: PROCEDURES FOR APPEAL OF A DENIAL

Section
1076.300   Appeal of a Denial
1076.310   Director's Response to Appeal

SUBPART E: PROCEDURES FOR PROVIDING PUBLIC RECORDS TO REQUESTORS

Section
1076.400   Inspection of Records at Department Offices
1076.410   Copies of Public Records; Copy Fees
1076.420   General Materials Available from the Freedom of Information Officer

APPENDIX A   Freedom of Information Request Form (Repealed)
APPENDIX B   Fee Schedule for Duplication of Public Records (Repealed)

AUTHORITY: Implementing and authorized by the Freedom of Information Act [5 ILCS 140] and Section 5-15 of the Illinois Administrative Procedure Act [5 ILCS 100/5-15].

SOURCE: Adopted at 8 Ill. Reg. 12322, effective July 2, 1984; amended at 13 Ill. Reg. 7940, effective May 16, 1989; amended at 23 Ill. Reg. _____,

---

ILLINOIS REGISTER 2740

DEPARTMENT OF NUCLEAR SAFETY

NOTICE OF PROPOSED AMENDMENTS

effective _____.

SUBPART A: INTRODUCTION

Section 1076.10 Summary and Purpose

a) This Part part is established to implement the provisions of the Freedom of Information Act [5 ILCS 140] (Supp. to Ill. Rev. Stat. 1983, ch. 116, par. 201 et seq.). The purpose of this Part these rules is to support the policy of providing public access to the public records in the possession of the Department of Nuclear Safety while, at the same time, protecting legitimate privacy interests and maintaining administrative efficiency.

b) This Part establishes a These rules establish the procedure by which the public may request and obtain public records of the Department of Nuclear Safety. This Part The rules also sets set forth the procedures to be followed by the Department in responding to requests for information.

(Source: Amended at 23 Ill. Reg. _____, effective _____)

Section 1076.20 Definitions

a) Terms used in this Part these rules shall have the same meaning as in the Freedom of Information Act.

b) The following definitions are applicable for purposes of this Part these rules:

"Department" means the Department of Nuclear Safety.

"Director" means the Director of the Department of Nuclear Safety.

"FOIA" means the Freedom of Information Act.

"Freedom of Information Officer" or "FOI Officer" means an individual responsible for receiving and responding to requests for public records.

"Requestor" means a person who submits a request for public records in accordance with this Part these rules.

"Working days" means calendar days other than Saturdays, Sundays and legal holidays.

(Source: Amended at 23 Ill. Reg. _____, effective _____)

DEPARTMENT OF NUCLEAR SAFETY

NOTICE OF PROPOSED AMENDMENTS

SUBPART B: PROCEDURES FOR REQUESTING PUBLIC RECORDS

Section 1076.100 Person To Whom Requests Are Submitted

Requests All requests for public records shall be submitted to the Department's Freedom of Information Officer either by mail (postal service or express mail) or telefax as follows at the following address:

a) Mail at the following address:

Freedom of Information Officer
Illinois Department of Nuclear Safety
1035 Outer Park Drive
Springfield, Illinois 62704

ATTN: FOIA Request

b) Telefax as follows:

Freedom of Information Officer
Illinois Department of Nuclear Safety
Telefax No. (217) 524-3698
ATTN: FOIA Request

(Source: Amended at 23 Ill. Reg. _____, effective _____)

Section 1076.110 Form and Content of Requests

a) All requests for public records submitted to the Department under the FOIA shall be in writing and signed by the requestor.
b) The requestor shall include the following information in any request for public records:
1) The requestor's full name, mailing address and telephone number, including area code, at which the requestor can be reached during normal business hours.
2) A description of the public records sought, being as specific as possible.
3) Whether the request is for inspection of public records, copies of public records, or both.

(Source: Amended at 23 Ill. Reg. _____, effective _____)

SUBPART C: PROCEDURES FOR DEPARTMENT RESPONSE TO REQUESTS FOR PUBLIC RECORDS

Section 1076.200 Timeline for Department Response

DEPARTMENT OF NUCLEAR SAFETY

NOTICE OF PROPOSED AMENDMENTS

a) The Department shall respond to a written request for public records within 7 seven working days after the receipt of such request by the Freedom of Information Officer.
b) In the event that the Department cannot respond to the request for public records within 7 seven working days for one of the reasons provided in Section 3(d) of the FOIA [5 ILCS 140/3(d)], the Department shall have an additional 7 seven working days in which to respond. The Department shall give the requestor notice of the extension of time to respond. Such notice of extension shall set forth the reasons why the extension is necessary.

(Source: Amended at 23 Ill. Reg. _____, effective _____)

Section 1076.210 Types of Department Responses

a) The Department shall respond to a request for public records in one of three ways:
1) Approve the request.
2) Approve in part and deny in part.
3) Deny the request.
b) When a request for public records has been approved, the Department shall may give notice that the requested material will be made available upon receipt of payment from the requestor for of reproduction costs and postage charges, or give notice of the time and place for inspection of the requested material.
c) Requests for public records shall be denied only for the reasons stated in either Section 3(f) or Section 7 of the FOIA [5 ILCS 140/3 and 7]. A denial of a request shall be made in writing and shall provide the reasons for the denial, the names and titles of individuals responsible for the decision to deny the request, and a statement that the requestor may appeal the denial to the Department of Nuclear Safety.
d) Categorical requests creating an undue burden upon the Department shall be denied only after extending to the requestor an opportunity to narrow the request to manageable proportions in accordance with Section 3(f) of the FOIA [5 ILCS 140/3(f)].
e) Failure to respond to a written request within 7 seven working days may be considered by the requestor as a denial of the request. Such a denial may be appealed to the Director in accordance with Section 1076.230 of this Part.

(Source: Amended at 23 Ill. Reg. _____, effective _____)

SUBPART D: PROCEDURES FOR APPEAL OF A DENIAL

Section 1076.300 Appeal of a Denial

ILLINOIS REGISTER 2743
99

DEPARTMENT OF NUCLEAR SAFETY

NOTICE OF PROPOSED AMENDMENTS

a) A requestor whose request for public records has been denied by the
Freedom of Information Officer may appeal the denial to the Director
of the Department. The appeal must be received by the Department
either by mail (postal service or express mail) or telefax within 10
working days after the date of the denial. The notice of appeal shall
be made in writing and shall be addressed to:

Director
Illinois Department of Nuclear Safety
1035 Outer Park Drive
Springfield, Illinois 62704
ATTN: FOIA APPEAL

b) The notice of appeal shall include a copy of the original request, a
copy of the denial received by the requestor or a statement that the
Department failed to respond to the requestor within 7 seven working
days, and a written statement setting forth the reasons why the
requestor believes the appeal should be granted.

(Source: Amended at 23 Ill. Reg. _____, effective
_____)

Section 1076.310 Director's Response to Appeal

The Director shall respond to an appeal within 7 seven working days after
receiving notice of the appeal thereof. The Director shall either affirm the
denial or provide access to the requested public records. Failure of the
Director to respond within 7 seven working days may be considered by the
requestor an affirmation of the denial. The Director's response shall state
the requestor's right to a judicial review of the decision pursuant to Section
11 of the FOIA [5 ILCS 140/11].

(Source: Amended at 23 Ill. Reg. _____, effective
_____)

SUBPART E: PROCEDURES FOR PROVIDING PUBLIC RECORDS TO REQUESTORS

Section 1076.400 Inspection of Records at Department Offices

a) Generally, public records will be made available for inspection at the
Department's Springfield offices between the hours of 8:30 a.m. and
5:00 p.m., Monday through Friday, except on State state holidays. A
place will be provided in which the requestor may inspect public
records.

b) Files shall be reviewed and exempt or confidential information shall
be deleted by the FOI Officer before a requestor is permitted access
to the records.

c) The requestor shall arrange a time and date with the FOI Officer to

ILLINOIS REGISTER 2744
99

DEPARTMENT OF NUCLEAR SAFETY

NOTICE OF PROPOSED AMENDMENTS

review records.
d)b) Documents that which the requestor wishes to have copied shall be
segregated during the course of the inspection. Generally, all
copying will be done by Department employees.
e)c) A requestor shall not be permitted to take a brief case, folder or
other similar materials or pens into the room in which the inspection
will take place. A requestor will be permitted to take pencil and
paper into the room while inspecting public records.
f)d) An employee of the Department may be present throughout the
inspection.
g) The requestor may not remove records from the Department offices,
except those copies produced and paid for (if applicable per Section
1076.410 of this Part) during the requestor's inspection of the files.

(Source: Amended at 23 Ill. Reg. _____, effective
_____)

Section 1076.410 Copies of Public Records; Copy Fees

a) Copies of public records shall be provided to the requestor only upon
payment of any charges which are due. If payment is not received
within 60 days after the Department has notified the requestor of the
charge, the Department shall consider the request withdrawn. The
Department shall notify the requestor in writing that the request has
been withdrawn.
b) Fees Charges for copies of public records on letter or legal size
paper shall be calculated at the rate of 35 cents per page assessed in
accordance with the "Fee Schedule for Duplication of public Records"
set forth in Appendix B of this Part. If the requestor asks that
copies of the public records be sent to the requestor him, postal or
express mail charges shall be assessed at the actual rate charged to
the Department.
c) Fees for document reproduction requests that require creation of
computer programs and computer generated records, or copying of
microfilmed or electronically imaged information, shall be based on
actual costs incurred by the Department.
d) The Department may provide information on diskette in an electronic
form such as an ASCII comma delimited file. The fee for such material
will be based on the actual cost incurred by the Department.
e) Some records possessed by the Department are in book or pamphlet form.
A fee may be assessed for such materials based on the actual cost
incurred by the Department.
f) Fees for reproducing records in a form not listed in this Section
(e.g., computer tapes, printouts, video tapes, maps and blueprints)
will be based on the actual costs incurred by the Department.
g) There shall be no fee charged for inspection of records or the
Department's costs in searching for and reviewing records.
h) Payment shall be remitted by check or money order, made payable to the

DEPARTMENT OF NUCLEAR SAFETY

NOTICE OF PROPOSED AMENDMENTS

Department of Nuclear Safety, and shall be sent to the Freedom of Information Officer.
1) Fees for certification of records shall be $2 per certification.
1)e) Fees charges shall be waived if:
   1) the requestor is a State agency,
   2) the requestor is a constitutional officer or a member of the General Assembly,
   3) the requestor states the specific purpose for the request and indicates that a waiver of the fee is in the public interest. Waiver of the fee is in the public interest if the principal purpose of the request is to access and disseminate information regarding the health, safety and welfare or the legal rights of the general public and is not for the principal purpose of personal or commercial benefit (Section 6(b) of the FOIA [5 ILCS 140/6(b)]) as amended by P.A. 85-1357, effective January 1, 1989), or
   4) the total charge for copies of the public records, including any postal charges and any fees assessed in accordance with this Section the "Fee Schedule for Duplication of Public Records," set forth in Appendix B, is less than $10 ten dollars.

(Source: Amended at 23 Ill. Reg. _____, effective

DEPARTMENT OF NUCLEAR SAFETY

NOTICE OF PROPOSED AMENDMENTS

Section 1076.APPENDIX B Fee Schedule for Duplication of Public Records (Repealed)

Type of Duplication	Per Copy Charge
Paper copy from paper original	$ .04
(possibly different charges for different sizes)	--
Computer printout paper per page	.50
Address labels (per label)	$ .03

Some records possessed by the Department are in book or pamphlet form. A charge may be assessed for such materials based upon the cost of such materials incurred by the Department.

The fees for reproducing records in a form not listed above (e.g., computer tapes, video tapes, maps, etc.) will be the actual cost of reproducing such records incurred by the Department.

(Source: Repealed at 23 Ill. Reg. _____, effective _____)

ILLINOIS REGISTER 2747
99

BOARD OF HIGHER EDUCATION

NOTICE OF ADOPTED RULES

1) Heading of the Part: State Matching Grant Program

2) Code Citation: 23 Ill. Adm. Code 1038

3)
Section Numbers:	Adopted Action:
1038.10	New Section
1038.20	New Section
1038.30	New Section
1038.40	New Section
1038.50	New Section
1038.60	New Section
1038.70	New Section

4) Statutory Authority: Implementing and authorized by 110 ILCS 205/9.26

5) Effective Date of Rules: February 17, 1999

6) Does this rulemaking contain an automatic repeal date? No

7) Does this rulemaking contain incorporations by reference? Yes

8) A copy of the adopted rule, including any material incorporated by reference, is on file in the agency's principal office and is available for public inspection.

9) Notice of Proposal Published in Illinois Register: October 23, 1998, 22 Ill. Reg. 19151

10) Has JCAR issued a Statement of Objection to these rules? No

11) Difference(s) between proposal and final version:

Section 1038.50(c)(2)(A)   research projects and matching contributions listed in the application comply with ~~administrative rules~~ this Part;

Section 1038.50(c)(2)(D)   the institution will refund to the Board of Higher Education the prorated amount of any grant funds for matched projects for which funding is not received, for which matching or grant funds are not properly expended, or for which the institution is deemed ineligible; and

Section 1038.50(d)   Application information may be obtained from and shall be submitted to:

> State Matching Grant Program
> Illinois Board of Higher Education
> 4 West Old Capitol Plaza, Room 500
> Springfield, Illinois 62701

ILLINOIS REGISTER 2748
99

BOARD OF HIGHER EDUCATION

NOTICE OF ADOPTED RULES

217/782-7184

Section 1038.70(b)   Audit. Each recipient of a State Matching Grant Program grant shall submit an audit performed by an external auditor who is registered as a public accountant by the Illinois Department of Professional Regulation. Such audit shall include a report from the auditor as to whether, for each identified project, sponsor research funds were received during the matching period and the institutional matching contributions were truly stated based on conditions and assurances included in the State Matching Grant Program grant application and award letter. The auditor also shall report as to whether grant funds were expended in accordance with the uses outlined in Section 1038.60. A State Matching Grant Program grant specific audit is required and shall he performed in accordance with Government Auditing Standards, 1994 Revision, issued by the United States General Accounting Office, Comptroller General of the United States. Audits are due by October 1 following the end of the expenditure period.

The Government Auditing Standards, 1994 Revision, is offered for sale by the U.S. Government Printing Office, Superintendent of Documents, Mail Stop: SSOP, Washington, DC 20402-9328, ISBN 0-16-045011-X.) A copy of this publication is on file at the Board of Higher Education Office.

One change was made in response to an oral discussion with a representative from Northwestern University for clarification in the definition for "matched project". That clarification is as follows:

"Matched project" means a sponsored research project for which an award was paid to the institution made by an external sponsor during the matching period, for which the institution made a required matching contribution, and which meets the project eligibility criteria set forth in Section 1038.30.

12) Have all the changes agreed upon by the agency and JCAR been made as indicated in the agreements issued by JCAR? Yes

13) Will this rule replace an emergency rule currently in effect? No

14) Are there any amendments pending on this Part? No

15) Summary and Purpose of Rule: The rules implement a grant program designed to strengthen research capabilities of Illinois higher education institutions and to draw additional research dollars to those institutions for purposes of increasing those capabilities.

16) Information and questions regarding this adopted rule shall be directed to:

BOARD OF HIGHER EDUCATION

NOTICE OF ADOPTED RULES

Carolyn Lorton, Associate Director
Illinois Board of Higher Education
4 West Old Capitol Plaza, Room 500
Springfield, Illinois 62701-1287
217/782-2551 or lorton@ibhe.state.il.us

The full text of the Adopted Rules begins on the next page:

BOARD OF HIGHER EDUCATION

NOTICE OF ADOPTED RULES

TITLE 23: EDUCATION AND CULTURAL RESOURCES
SUBTITLE A: EDUCATION
CHAPTER II: BOARD OF HIGHER EDUCATION

PART 1038
STATE MATCHING GRANT PROGRAM

Section
1038.10   Purpose
1038.20   Definitions
1038.30   Project Eligibility Criteria
1038.40   Funding Formula
1038.50   Application Requirements for Determination of Grant Funds Allocation
1038.60   Use of Grant Funds
1038.70   Conditions and Administrative Responsibilities

AUTHORITY: Implementing and authorized by Section 9.26 of the Board of Higher Education Act [110 ILCS 205/9.26].

SOURCE: Adopted at 23 Ill. Reg. 2715733, effective FEB 17 1999.

Section 1038.10 Purpose

The purpose of this Part is to provide for the distribution of matching grants to Illinois institutions of higher education as incentives in the competition for external grants and contracts. Grants will be made to stimulate increased federal and corporate research funds and to improve the research capabilities of those institutions. [110 ILCS 205/9.26]

Section 1038.20 Definitions

"Applied research" means systematic study and investigation undertaken to discover the applications and uses of knowledge and principles in actual work or in solving problems.

"Basic research" means systematic study and investigation undertaken to discover new knowledge and establish facts or principles.

"Board" means the Illinois Board of Higher Education.

"Expenditure period" means the two-year period beginning on the first day of the grant period.

"Grant funds" means dollars appropriated by the State of Illinois to be used in support of the State Matching Grant Program.

ILLINOIS REGISTER 2751

BOARD OF HIGHER EDUCATION

NOTICE OF ADOPTED RULES

"Grant period" means the State of Illinois fiscal year for which grant funds are appropriated.

"Institution" means an Illinois public university or community college, or not-for-profit degree-granting independent college or university.

"Matched project" means a sponsored research project for which an award was paid to the institution by an external sponsor during the matching period, for which the institution made a required matching contribution, and that meets the project eligibility criteria set forth in Section 1038.30.

"Matching contribution" is the institution's resource commitment to a sponsored research project as required by the terms of the agreement between the institution and the project sponsor. Matching contributions shall not include the contributed effort of project investigators and shall be limited to institutionally-provided direct costs separately budgeted and accounted for as the institution's contribution to the research project.

"Matching period" means the State of Illinois fiscal year immediately preceding the State fiscal year for which grant funds are appropriated.

"Sponsor" means an entity, other than the State of Illinois, the applicant institution, or any consortium in which the institution is a member, that provides primary financial support for research project activities.

"Supported project" means a sponsored research project for which an award is formally committed to by an external sponsor, for which the receipt of sponsored research grant funding requires an institutional matching contribution, that meets the criteria set forth in Section 1038.30, and for which grant funds will be allocated to meet all or part of the matching contribution during the expenditure period. Multi-year projects may be submitted for only one year at a time, but may be re-submitted annually during the life of the project if the project sponsor is required to make a re-determination each year that the institution is eligible for grant funding.

Section 1038.30 Project Eligibility Criteria

Projects shall meet the following criteria to be eligible for inclusion as a matched project in the grant application or as a supported project for which grant funds will be used.

a) The project is a research project and is described by the sponsor as a research project.

ILLINOIS REGISTER 2752

BOARD OF HIGHER EDUCATION

NOTICE OF ADOPTED RULES

b) The research project is awarded grant funds through an open and competitive process of merit review.

c) Matching funds are required by the sponsor under the terms of the award or the award is conditioned on a match as a determination of institutional commitment.

d) The institution is committed to provide a specified matching contribution and shall provide funding for any portion of the matching contribution not covered by the State Matching Grant Program.

e) Projects must be basic research or applied research activities.

f) Such activities as training of personnel, workforce training or development, curricular research or development, clinical trials, or building construction or renovation (except for renovation costs incurred in support of an eligible project) shall be only incidental to the basic research or applied research activities.

g) Research projects for which the State of Illinois has provided a specific grant or appropriation are ineligible for matching funds under this grant program. However, research projects for which State Matching Grant Program grants or other State funds were used as matching contributions during the matching period are eligible for inclusion as a matched project in establishing the subsequent year's allocation base.

h) The results of the sponsored research project must be available to the public or to the sponsoring governmental agency. Research projects may not support private, non-governmental, or for-profit research activities.

Section 1038.40 Funding Formula

State Matching Grant Program grant funds shall be allocated to each participating institution based on the institution's total sponsored grant funding for eligible matched projects received during the matching period as a proportion of the total sponsor grant funding for matched projects received during the matching period for all institutions submitting grant applications. In this formula, funds provided to any third party as a subawardee are to be excluded.

Section 1038.50 Application Requirements for Determination of Grant Funds Allocation

a) The Board shall notify in writing the chief executive officer of every institution in the State of Illinois of the availability of grant funds not less than 45 days before the deadline for submission of applications.

b) Applications must be completed on forms prescribed by the Board.

c) Grant funds applications shall contain, at a minimum:
   1) For each matched project, the following information:
      A) project title;
      B) copy of official award notification;

BOARD OF HIGHER EDUCATION

NOTICE OF ADOPTED RULES

C) total grant funding and grant funding received during the matching period (less grant funds provided to a subgrantee during the matching period); and
D) a description of specific institutional matching requirements and matching contributions expended during the matching period.
2) Certification by the chief executive officer of the institution that:
A) research projects and matching contributions listed in the application comply with this Part;
B) the institution will provide a program specific audit as required by this Part;
C) the institution will comply with this Part and applicable State and federal statutes;
D) the institution will refund to the Board of Higher Education the prorated amount of grant funds for matched projects for which funding is not received, for which matching or grant funds are not properly expended, or for which the institution is deemed ineligible; and
E) the institution will provide such additional information requested by the Board or external evaluators as necessary to administer this program.
d) Application information may be obtained from, and applications shall be submitted to:

State Matching Grant Program
Illinois Board of Higher Education
4 West Old Capitol Plaza, Room 500
Springfield, Illinois 62701
217/782-7184

Section 1038.60 Use of Grant Funds

a) State Matching Grant Program grant funds may be used for:
1) All or part of the institution's required matching contribution during the grant expenditure period for eligible sponsored research projects for which the institution receives formal notification of the awarding of sponsor research funds during the grant period.
2) Audit of grant funds.
b) The Board will distribute grant funds to institutions based on:
1) The institution's allocation of grant funds as determined in Section 1038.40, one-half of which will be distributed to grant recipients at the time of allocation.
2) The remainder of the institution's allocation after the Board receives a request for the distribution of the remaining grant funds from the institution that includes a listing of all newly eligible sponsored research projects for which the institution

BOARD OF HIGHER EDUCATION

NOTICE OF ADOPTED RULES

received award notification during the grant period and copies of the formal award notification letters from the project sponsors.

Section 1038.70 Conditions and Administrative Responsibilities

a) Non-Discrimination. No recipient shall discriminate on the basis of race, creed, sex, handicap, color, or national origin in the employment, training, or promotion of personnel.
b) Audit. Each recipient of a State Matching Grant Program grant shall submit an audit performed by an external auditor who is certified as a public accountant by the Illinois Department of Professional Regulation. Such audit shall include a report from the auditor as to whether, for each identified project, sponsor research funds were received during the matching period and the institutional matching contributions were truly stated based on conditions and assurances included in the State Matching Grant Program grant application and award letter. The auditor also shall report as to whether grant funds were expended in accordance with the uses outlined in Section 1038.60. A State Matching Grant Program grant specific audit is required and shall be performed in accordance with Government Auditing Standards, 1994 Revision, issued by the United States General Accounting Office, Comptroller General of the United States. Audits are due by October 1 following the end of the expenditure period.
The Government Accounting Standards, 1994 Revision, is offered for sale by the U.S. Government Printing Office, Superintendent of Documents, Mail Stop: SSOP, Washington, DC 20402-9328, ISBN 0-16-045011-X. A copy of this publication is on file at the Board of Higher Education Office.
c) Evaluation Report. A report documenting the external leveraging of funds achieved and results achieved by the matching grant funds is to be provided. The report shall document the extent to which the institutions' ability to attract funds has been enhanced by the State Matching Grant Program and what monetary and non-monetary benefits have accrued to the citizens of Illinois as a result of projects included in the State Matching Grant Program. Evaluation reports are due October 1 following the end of the expenditure period.
d) Any matched project that was used to obtain grant funds, but for which sponsor funding was never received, for any reason, shall require a prorated return of the grant funds attributed to that project.
e) Grant funds not expended as matching contributions for eligible projects identified by the grant recipient shall be refunded to the Board.
f) With the assistance of a panel of external evaluators, the State Matching Grant Program will be reviewed annually and the results reported to the Board of Higher Education. The following questions will be addressed in the report:
1) To what extent have the objectives of the program been achieved?
2) How many federal and corporate research dollars have come to

ILLINOIS REGISTER 2756

F HIGHER EDUCATION

OF ADOPTED RULES

of projects included in the program?
non-monetary benefits have accrued to the
as a result of the projects supported by the

POLLUTION CONTROL BOARD

NOTICE OF ADOPTED AMENDMENTS

1) Heading of the Part: Primary Drinking Water Standards

2) Code Citation: 35 Ill. Adm. Code 611

3) Section Numbers: Adopted Action:
   611.101   Amended
   611.102   Amended
   611.126   Amended
   611.290   Amended

4) Statutory Authority: 415 ILCS 5/17.5 and 27

5) Effective date of amendments: February 17, 1999

6) Does this rulemaking contain an automatic repeal date? No

7) Do these amendments contain incorporations by reference? Yes. Section
   611.102 is the central listing of all documents incorporated by reference
   throughout Part 611. Included among the amendments is the addition of an
   incorporation of NSF Standard 61, section 9 by reference for the purposes
   of Section 611.126(b)(3). The Board has also used this opportunity to
   update the version of the *Code of Federal Regulations* incorporated to the
   1998 edition, which is now available.

8) The adopted amendments, a copy of the Board's opinion and order adopted
   February 4, 1999, and all materials incorporated by reference are on file
   at the Board's principal office and are available for public inspection
   and copying.

9) Notice of proposal published in Illinois Register: December 11, 1998, 22
   Ill. Reg. 21239

)10 Has JCAR issued a Statement of Objections to these rules? No. Section
    17.5 of the Environmental Protection Act [415 ILCS 5/17.5] provides that
    Section 5 of the Illinois Administrative Procedure Act [5 ILCS 100/5-35
    and 5-40] shall not apply. Because this rulemaking is not subject to
    Section 5 of the IAPA, it is not subject to first notice or to second
    notice review by JCAR.

11) Differences between proposal and final version: The Board did not make
    significant changes in the text of the proposed amendments. We did,
    however, make a number of minor changes at the suggestion of JCAR or on
    our own initiative. The alterations are listed in the following table:

POLLUTION CONTROL BOARD

NOTICE OF ADOPTED AMENDMENTS

Revisions to the Text of the Proposed Amendments in Final Adoption

Section Revised	Source(s) of Revision(s)	Revision(s)
611.101 "Approved source of bottled water"	JCAR	Corrected "U.S.C." to "USC"; removed section symbols
611.101 "Best available technology"	JCAR	Corrected "U.S. EPA" to "USEPA"
611.101 "Best available technology"	JCAR	Corrected "U.S. EPA" to "USEPA"
611.101 "Phase I"	JCAR	Corrected "U.S. EPA" to "USEPA"
611.101 "Phase II"	JCAR	Corrected "U.S. EPA" to "USEPA"
611.101 "Phase IIB"	JCAR	Corrected "U.S. EPA" to "USEPA"
611.101 "Phase V"	JCAR	Corrected "U.S. EPA" to "USEPA"
611.101 "public water system"	JCAR	Corrected ending punctuation of first subparagraph to a semicolon; removed unnecessary ending semicolon
611.101 "Safe Drinking Water Act"	JCAR	Corrected "U.S.C." to "USC"
611.101 "service connection" Board note	JCAR	Corrected "U.S.C." to "USC"; removed section symbol
611.101 "special irrigation district" Board note	JCAR	Corrected "U.S.C." to "USC"; removed section symbol
611.101 "total trihalomethanes" Board note	JCAR	Corrected "U.S. EPA" to "USEPA"
611.101 "transient, non-community water system"	JCAR	Corrected "U.S.C." to "USC"; removed section symbol
611.101 "USEPA"	JCAR, Board	Added "USEPA or"
611.101 "VOC"	JCAR	Corrected "U.S. EPA" to "USEPA"
611.101 "wellness protection program"	JCAR	Corrected "U.S. EPA" to "USEPA"
611.102(b) "NSF"	Board	Corrected telephone area code; corrected edition of NSF standard 61 incorporated by reference to the current edition
611.126(a)	JCAR	Removed comma after date "1986"
611.126(b)(3)	JCAR	Capitalized "when"; corrected "U.S.C." to "USC"; removed section symbol

12) **Have all the changes agreed upon by the Board and JCAR been made as indicated in the agreements issued by JCAR?** Section 17.5 of the Environmental Protection Act provides that Section 5 of the Administrative Procedure Act shall not apply. Because this rulemaking is not subject to Section 5 of the IAPA, it is not subject to first notice or to second notice review by JCAR.

13) **Will these amendments replace emergency amendments currently in effect?** No

14) **Are there any other amendments pending on this Part?** No

15) **Summary and purpose of amendments:** A more detailed description is contained in the Board's opinion and order of February 4, 1999, in R99-6, which opinion and order is available from the address below. Section 17.5 of the Environmental Protection Act provides that Section 5 of the Illinois Administrative Procedure Act shall not apply. Because this rulemaking is not subject to Section 5 of the IAPA, it is not subject to first notice or to second notice review by JCAR.

The R99-6 proceeding updates the Board's SDWA drinking water regulations to correspond with amendments adopted by USEPA that appeared in the Federal Register during the period January 1, 1998, through June 30, 1998. During that time, USEPA amended the federal SDWA regulations twice, summarized as follows:

63 Fed. Reg. 23361 (April 28, 1998):
USEPA adopted amendments to the requirements for authorization of state SDWA programs, i.e., the state primacy requirements. The primary aspects of this action relate to state civil penalty authority, the time within which the state must adopt amendments corresponding to federal amendments, and the primacy status of the state pending a final USEPA determination on its primacy application. Accompanying amendments clarify the NPDWR definition of

ILLINOIS REGISTER 2759

POLLUTION CONTROL BOARD

NOTICE OF ADOPTED AMENDMENTS

"non-community water system", expand the definition of "public water system", and add a definition of "service connection".

63 Fed. Reg. 31932 (June 11, 1998)
USEPA adopted amendments that allow the use of point-of-entry devices to meet the NPDWRs. USEPA did this by removing the prohibition against doing so.

In addition to the amendments that are driven by USEPA amendments to the NPDWRs, the Board has added amendments derived from a federal statutory amendment. Those amendments are derived from amendments to section 1417(a) of SDWA (42 USC Section 300g-6(a) (1996)) made by Congress in the 1986 SDWA amendments (Pub. L. 104-182, Title I, Section 118, 110 Stat. 1645, 1691) that prohibit the use of lead-containing fixtures.

16) Information and questions regarding these adopted amendments shall be directed to:

Michael J. McCambridge
Attorney
Illinois Pollution Control Board
100 W. Randolph 11-500
Chicago IL 60601
312-814-6924

Request copies of the Board's opinion and order of February 4, 1999, from the Clerk of the Board at 312-814-3620.

The full text of the adopted amendments begins on the next page:

ILLINOIS REGISTER 2760

POLLUTION CONTROL BOARD

NOTICE OF ADOPTED AMENDMENTS

TITLE 35: ENVIRONMENTAL PROTECTION
SUBTITLE F: PUBLIC WATER SUPPLIES
CHAPTER I: POLLUTION CONTROL BOARD

PART 611
PRIMARY DRINKING WATER STANDARDS

SUBPART A: GENERAL

Section
611.100   Purpose, Scope and Applicability
611.101   Definitions
611.102   Incorporations by Reference
611.103   Severability
611.107   Agency Inspection of PWS Facilities
611.108   Delegation to Local Government
611.109   Enforcement
611.110   Special Exception Permits
611.111   Section 1415 Variances
611.112   Section 1416 Variances
611.113   Alternative Treatment Techniques
611.114   Siting Requirements
611.115   Source Water Quantity
611.120   Effective dates
611.121   Maximum Contaminant Levels and Finished Water Quality
611.125   Fluoridation Requirement
611.126   Prohibition on Use of Lead
611.130   Special Requirements for Certain Variances and Adjusted Standards

SUBPART B: FILTRATION AND DISINFECTION

Section
611.201   Requiring a Demonstration
611.202   Procedures for Agency Determinations
611.211   Filtration Required
611.212   Groundwater under Direct Influence of Surface Water
611.213   No Method of HPC Analysis
611.220   General Requirements
611.230   Filtration Effective Dates
611.231   Source Water Quality Conditions
611.232   Site-specific Conditions
611.233   Treatment Technique Violations
611.240   Disinfection
611.241   Unfiltered PWSs
611.242   Filtered PWSs
611.250   Filtration
611.261   Unfiltered PWSs: Reporting and Recordkeeping
611.262   Filtered PWSs: Reporting and Recordkeeping

POLLUTION CONTROL BOARD

NOTICE OF ADOPTED AMENDMENTS

611.271	Protection during Repair Work
611.272	Disinfection following Repair

SUBPART C: USE OF NON-CENTRALIZED TREATMENT DEVICES

Section
611.280	Point-of-Entry Devices
611.290	Use of Point-of-Use Devices or Bottled Water

SUBPART D: TREATMENT TECHNIQUES

Section
611.295	General Requirements
611.296	Acrylamide and Epichlorohydrin
611.297	Corrosion Control

SUBPART F: MAXIMUM CONTAMINANT LEVELS (MCL's)

Section
611.300	Old MCLs for Inorganic Chemicals
611.301	Revised MCLs for Inorganic Chemicals
611.310	Old MCLs for Organic Chemicals
611.311	Revised MCLs for Organic Contaminants
611.320	Turbidity
611.325	Microbiological Contaminants
611.330	Radium and Gross Alpha Particle Activity
611.331	Beta Particle and Photon Radioactivity

SUBPART G: LEAD AND COPPER

Section
611.350	General Requirements
611.351	Applicability of Corrosion Control
611.352	Corrosion Control Treatment
611.353	Source Water Treatment
611.354	Lead Service Line Replacement
611.355	Public Education and Supplemental Monitoring
611.356	Tap Water Monitoring for Lead and Copper
611.357	Monitoring for Water Quality Parameters
611.358	Monitoring for Lead and Copper in Source Water
611.359	Analytical Methods
611.360	Reporting
611.361	Recordkeeping

SUBPART R: GENERAL MONITORING AND ANALYTICAL REQUIREMENTS

Section
611.480	Alternative Analytical Techniques

611.490	Certified Laboratories
611.491	Laboratory Testing Equipment
611.500	Consecutive PWSs
611.510	Special Monitoring for Unregulated Contaminants

SUBPART L: MICROBIOLOGICAL MONITORING AND ANALYTICAL REQUIREMENTS

Section
611.521	Routine Coliform Monitoring
611.522	Repeat Coliform Monitoring
611.523	Invalidation of Total Coliform Samples
611.524	Sanitary Surveys
611.525	Fecal Coliform and E. Coli Testing
611.526	Analytical Methodology
611.527	Response to Violation
611.531	Analytical Requirements
611.532	Unfiltered PWSs
611.533	Filtered PWSs

SUBPART M: TURBIDITY MONITORING AND ANALYTICAL REQUIREMENTS

Section
611.560	Turbidity

SUBPART N: INORGANIC MONITORING AND ANALYTICAL REQUIREMENTS

Section
611.591	Violation of State MCL
611.592	Frequency of State Monitoring
611.600	Applicability
611.601	Monitoring Frequency
611.602	Asbestos Monitoring Frequency
611.603	Inorganic Monitoring Frequency
611.604	Nitrate Monitoring
611.605	Nitrite Monitoring
611.606	Confirmation Samples
611.607	More Frequent Monitoring and Confirmation Sampling
611.608	Additional Optional Monitoring
611.609	Determining Compliance
611.610	Inorganic Monitoring Times
611.611	Inorganic Analysis
611.612	Monitoring Requirements for Old Inorganic MCLs
611.630	Special Monitoring for Sodium
611.631	Special Monitoring for Inorganic Chemicals

SUBPART O: ORGANIC MONITORING AND ANALYTICAL REQUIREMENTS

Section

POLLUTION CONTROL BOARD

NOTICE OF ADOPTED AMENDMENTS

611.640   Definitions
611.641   Old MCLs
611.645   Analytical Methods for Organic Chemical Contaminants
611.646   Phase I, Phase II, and Phase V Volatile Organic Contaminants
611.647   Sampling for Phase I Volatile Organic Contaminants (Repealed)
611.648   Phase II, Phase IIB, and Phase V Synthetic Organic Contaminants
611.650   Monitoring for 36 Contaminants (Repealed)
611.657   Analytical Methods for 36 Contaminants (Repealed)
611.658   Special Monitoring for Organic Chemicals

SUBPART P: THM MONITORING AND ANALYTICAL REQUIREMENTS

Section
611.680   Sampling, Analytical and other Requirements
611.683   Reduced Monitoring Frequency
611.684   Averaging
611.685   Analytical Methods
611.686   Modification to System
611.687   Sampling for THM Potential

SUBPART Q: RADIOLOGICAL MONITORING AND ANALYTICAL REQUIREMENTS

Section
611.720   Analytical Methods
611.731   Gross Alpha
611.732   Manmade Radioactivity

SUBPART T: REPORTING, PUBLIC NOTIFICATION AND RECORDKEEPING

Section
611.830   Applicability
611.831   Monthly Operating Report
611.832   Notice by Agency
611.833   Cross Connection Reporting
611.840   Reporting
611.851   Reporting MCL and other Violations
611.852   Reporting other Violations
611.853   Notice to New Billing Units
611.854   General Content of Public Notice
611.855   Mandatory Health Effects Language
611.856   Fluoride Notice
611.858   Fluoride Secondary Standard
611.860   Record Maintenance
611.870   List of 36 Contaminants

APPENDIX A   Mandatory Health Effects Information
APPENDIX B   Percent Inactivation of G. Lamblia Cysts
APPENDIX C   Common Names of Organic Chemicals

POLLUTION CONTROL BOARD

NOTICE OF ADOPTED AMENDMENTS

APPENDIX D   Defined Substrate Method for the Simultaneous Detection of
             Total Coliforms and Escherichia Coli from Drinking Water
APPENDIX E   Mandatory Lead Public Education Information
TABLE A   Total Coliform Monitoring Frequency
TABLE B   Fecal or Total Coliform Density Measurements
TABLE C   Frequency of RDC Measurement
TABLE D   Number of Lead and Copper Monitoring Sites
TABLE E   Lead and Copper Monitoring Start Dates
TABLE F   Number of Water Quality Parameter Sampling Sites
TABLE G   Summary of Monitoring Requirements for Water Quality Parameters
TABLE I   Federal Effective Dates

AUTHORITY: Implementing Sections 17 and 17.5 and authorized by Section 27 of
the Environmental Protection Act [415 ILCS 5/17, 17.5 and 27].

SOURCE: Adopted in R88-26 at 14 Ill. Reg. 16517, effective September 20, 1990;
amended in R90-21 at 14 Ill. Reg. 20448, effective December 11, 1990; amended
in R90-13 at 15 Ill. Reg. 1562, effective January 22, 1991; amended in R91-3 at
16 Ill. Reg. 19010, effective December 1, 1992; amended in R92-3 at 17 Ill.
Reg. 7796, effective May 18, 1993; amended in R93-1 at 17 Ill. Reg. 12650,
effective July 23, 1993; amended in R94-4 at 18 Ill. Reg. 12291, effective July
28, 1994; amended in R94-23 at 19 Ill. Reg. 8613, effective June 20, 1995;
amended in R95-17 at 20 Ill. Reg. 14493, effective October 22, 1996; amended in
R98-2 at 22 Ill. Reg. 5020, effective March 5, 1998; amended in R99-6 at 23
Ill. Reg. 2766 , effective FEB 17 1999   .

NOTE: In this Part, superscript numbers or letters are denoted by parentheses;
subscript are denoted by brackets.

SUBPART A: GENERAL

Section 611.101 Definitions

As used in this Part, the term:

    "Act" means the Environmental Protection Act [415 ILCS 5].

    "Agency" means the Illinois Environmental Protection Agency.
    BOARD NOTE: The Department of Public Health ("Public Health")
    regulates non-community water supplies ("non-CWSs", including
    non-transient, non-community water supplies ("NTNCWSs") and transient
    non-community water supplies ("transient non-CWSs")). For the
    purposes of regulation of supplies by Public Health by reference to
    this Part, "Agency" shall mean Public Health.

    "AI" means "inactivation ratio".

    "Approved sources of bottled water", for the purposes of Section

POLLUTION CONTROL BOARD

NOTICE OF ADOPTED AMENDMENTS

611.130(e)(4), means a source of water and the water therefrom; whether it be from a spring, artesian well, drilled well, municipal water supply, or any other source, that has been inspected and the water sampled, analyzed, and found to be a safe and sanitary quality according to applicable laws and regulations of State and local government agencies having jurisdiction, as evidenced by the presence in the plant of current certificates or notations of approval from each government agency or agencies having jurisdiction over the source, the water it bottles, and the distribution of the water in commerce.

BOARD NOTE: Derived from 40 CFR 142.62(g)(2) and 21 CFR 129.3(a) (1998+994). The Board cannot compile an exhausting listing of all federal, state, and local laws to which bottled water and bottling water may be subjected. However, the statutes and regulations of which the Board is aware are the following: the Illinois Food, Drug and Cosmetic Act (410 ILCS 620), the Bottled Water Act (815 ILCS 310), the DPH Water Well Construction Code (77 Ill. Adm. Code 920), the DPH Water Well Pump Installation Code (77 Ill. Adm. Code 925), the federal bottled water quality standards (21 CFR 103.35), the federal drinking water processing and bottling standards (21 CFR 129), the federal Good Manufacturing Practices for human foods (21 CFR 110), the federal Fair Packaging and Labeling Act (15 USC U.S.C. subsection 1451 et seq.), and the federal Fair Packaging and Labeling regulations (21 CFR 201).

"Best available technology" or "BAT" means the best technology, treatment techniques or other means that USEPA U.S. EPA has found are available for the contaminant in question. BAT is specified in Subpart F of this Part.

BOARD NOTE: Derived from 40 CFR 141.2 (1998+994).

"Board" means the Illinois Pollution Control Board.

"CAS No" means "Chemical Abstracts Services Number".

"CT" or "CT[calc]" is the product of "residual disinfectant concentration" (RDC or C) in mg/L determined before or at the first customer, and the corresponding "disinfectant contact time" (T) in minutes. If a supplier applies disinfectant at more than one point prior to the first customer, it shall determine the CT of each disinfectant sequence before or at the first customer to determine the total percent inactivation or "total inactivation ratio". In determining the total inactivation ratio, the supplier shall determine the RDC of each disinfection sequence and corresponding contact time before any subsequent disinfection application point(s). (See "CT[99.9]")

BOARD NOTE: Derived from 40 CFR 141.2 (1998+994).

ILLINOIS REGISTER 2766
99

POLLUTION CONTROL BOARD

NOTICE OF ADOPTED AMENDMENTS

"CT[99.9]" is the CT value required for 99.9 percent (3-log) inactivation of Giardia lamblia cysts. CT[99.9] for a variety of disinfectants and conditions appear in Tables 1.1-1.6, 2.1 and 3.1 of Section 611.Appendix B. (See "Inactivation Ratio".)

BOARD NOTE: Derived from the definition of CT in 40 CFR 141.2 (1998+994).

"Coagulation" means a process using coagulant chemicals and mixing by which colloidal and suspended materials are destabilized and agglomerated into flocs.

BOARD NOTE: Derived from 40 CFR 141.2 (1998+994).

"Community Water System" or "CWS" means a public water system (PWS) that serves at least 15 service connections used by year-round residents or regularly serves at least 25 year-round residents.

BOARD NOTE: Derived from 40 CFR 141.2 (1998+994). This definition differs slightly from that of Section 3.05 of the Act.

"Compliance cycle" means the nine-year calendar year cycle during which public water systems (PWSs) must monitor. Each compliance cycle consists of three three-year compliance periods. The first calendar cycle begins January 1, 1993, and ends December 31, 2001; the second begins January 1, 2002 and ends December 31, 2010; the third begins January 1, 2011, and ends December 31, 2019.

BOARD NOTE: Derived from 40 CFR 141.2 (1998+994).

"Compliance period" means a three-year calendar year period within a compliance cycle. Each compliance cycle has three three-year compliance periods. Within the first compliance cycle, the first compliance period runs from January 1, 1993, to December 31, 1995; the second from January 1, 1996, to December 31, 1998; the third from January 1, 1999, to December 31, 2001.

BOARD NOTE: Derived from 40 CFR 141.2 (1998+994).

"Confluent growth" means a continuous bacterial growth covering the entire filtration area of a membrane filter or a portion thereof, in which bacterial colonies are not discrete.

BOARD NOTE: Derived from 40 CFR 141.2 (1998+994).

"Contaminant" means any physical, chemical, biological or radiological substance or matter in water.

BOARD NOTE: Derived from 40 CFR 141.2 (1998+994).

"Conventional filtration treatment" means a series of processes including coagulation, flocculation, sedimentation and filtration resulting in substantial particulate removal.

BOARD NOTE: Derived from 40 CFR 141.2 (1998+994).

ILLINOIS REGISTER 2767
99

POLLUTION CONTROL BOARD

NOTICE OF ADOPTED AMENDMENTS

"Diatomaceous earth filtration" means a process resulting in substantial particulate removal in which:

A precoat cake of diatomaceous earth filter media is deposited on a support membrane (septum); and

While the water is filtered by passing through the cake on the septum, additional filter media known as body feed is continuously added to the feed water to maintain the permeability of the filter cake.
BOARD NOTE: Derived from 40 CFR 141.2 (1998+994).

"Direct filtration" means a series of processes including coagulation and filtration but excluding sedimentation resulting in substantial particulate removal.
BOARD NOTE: Derived from 40 CFR 141.2 (1998+994).

"Disinfectant" means any oxidant, including but not limited to chlorine, chlorine dioxide, chloramines and ozone added to water in any part of the treatment or distribution process, that is intended to kill or inactivate pathogenic microorganisms.
BOARD NOTE: Derived from 40 CFR 141.2 (1998+994).

"Disinfectant contact time" or "T" means the time in minutes that it takes for water to move from the point of disinfectant application or the previous point of RDC measurement to a point before or at the point where RDC ("C") is measured.

Where only one RDC is measured, T is the time in minutes that it takes for water to move from the point of disinfectant application to a point before or at where RDC is measured.

Where more than one RDC is measured, T is:

For the first measurement of RDC, the time in minutes that it takes for water to move from the first or only point of disinfectant application to a point before or at the point where the first RDC is measured and

For subsequent measurements of RDC, the time in minutes that it takes for water to move from the previous RDC measurement point for which the particular T is being calculated.

T in pipelines must be calculated based on "plug flow" by dividing the internal volume of the pipe by the maximum hourly flow rate through that pipe.

T within mixing basins and storage reservoirs must be determined

ILLINOIS REGISTER 2768
99

POLLUTION CONTROL BOARD

NOTICE OF ADOPTED AMENDMENTS

by tracer studies or an equivalent demonstration.
BOARD NOTE: Derived from 40 CFR 141.2 (1998+994).

"Disinfection" means a process that inactivates pathogenic organisms in water by chemical oxidants or equivalent agents.
BOARD NOTE: Derived from 40 CFR 141.2 (1998+994).

"Distribution system" includes all points downstream of an "entry point" to the point of consumer ownership.

"Domestic or other non-distribution system plumbing problem" means a coliform contamination problem in a PWS with more than one service connection that is limited to the specific service connection from which the coliform-positive sample was taken.
BOARD NOTE: Derived from 40 CFR 141.2 (1998+994).

"Dose equivalent" means the product of the absorbed dose from ionizing radiation and such factors as account for differences in biological effectiveness due to the type of radiation and its distribution in the body as specified by the International Commission on Radiological Units and Measurements (ICRU).
BOARD NOTE: Derived from 40 CFR 141.2 (1998+994).

"Entry point" means a point just downstream of the final treatment operation, but upstream of the first user and upstream of any mixing with other water. If raw water is used without treatment, the "entry point" is the raw water source. If a PWS receives treated water from another PWS, the "entry point" is a point just downstream of the other PWS, but upstream of the first user on the receiving PWS, and upstream of any mixing with other water.

"Filtration" means a process for removing particulate matter from water by passage through porous media.
BOARD NOTE: Derived from 40 CFR 141.2 (1998+994).

"Flocculation" means a process to enhance agglomeration or collection of smaller floc particles into larger, more easily settle able particles through gentle stirring by hydraulic or mechanical means.
BOARD NOTE: Derived from 40 CFR 141.2 (1998+994).

"GC" means "gas chromatography" or "gas-liquid phase chromatography".

"GC/MS" means gas chromatography (GC) followed by mass spectrometry (MS).

"Gross alpha particle activity" means the total radioactivity due to alpha particle emission as inferred from measurements on a dry sample.
BOARD NOTE: Derived from 40 CFR 141.2 (1998+994).

POLLUTION CONTROL BOARD

NOTICE OF ADOPTED AMENDMENTS

"Gross beta particle activity" means the total radioactivity due to alpha particle emission as inferred from measurements on a dry sample.
BOARD NOTE: Derived from 40 CFR 141.2 (1998↑994).

"Groundwater under the direct influence of surface water" is as determined in Section 611.212.
BOARD NOTE: Derived from 40 CFR 141.2 (1998↑994).

"GWS" means "groundwater system", a public water supply (PWS) that uses only groundwater sources.
BOARD NOTE: Drawn from 40 CFR 141.23(b)(2) & 141.24(f)(2) note (1998↑994).

"Halogen" means one of the chemical elements chlorine, bromine or iodine.
BOARD NOTE: Derived from 40 CFR 141.2 (1998↑994).

"HPC" means "heterotrophic plate count", measured as specified in Section 611.531(c).

"Inactivation Ratio" (Ai) means:

$$Ai = CT[calc]/CT[99.9]$$

The sum of the inactivation ratios, or "total inactivation ratio" (B) is calculated by adding together the inactivation ratio for each disinfection sequence:

$$B = SUM(Ai)$$

A total inactivation ratio equal to or greater than 1.0 is assumed to provide a 3-log inactivation of Giardia lamblia cysts.
BOARD NOTE: Derived from the definition of "CT" in 40 CFR 141.2 (1998↑994).

"Initial compliance period" means the three-year compliance period begins January 1, 1993, except for the MCLs for dichloromethane, 1,2,4-trichlorobenzene, 1,1, 2-trichloroethane, benzo[a]-pyrene, dalapon, di(2-ethylhexyl)adipate, di(2-ethylhexyl)- phthalate, dinoseb, diquat, endothall, endrin, glyphosate, hexachlorobenzene, hexachlorocyclopentadiene, oxamyl, picloram, simazine, 2,3,7,8-TCDD, antimony, beryllium, cyanide, nickel, and thallium as they apply to suppliers whose supplies have fewer than compliance period that begins on January 1, 1996.
BOARD NOTE: Derived from 40 CFR 141.2 (1998↑994).

"L" means "liter".

ILLINOIS REGISTER 2770

POLLUTION CONTROL BOARD

NOTICE OF ADOPTED AMENDMENTS

"Legionella" means a genus of bacteria, some species of which have caused a type of pneumonia called Legionnaires Disease.
BOARD NOTE: Derived from 40 CFR 141.2 (1998↑994).

"Man-made beta particle and photon emitters" means all radionuclides emitting beta particles and/or photons listed in Maximum Permissible Body Burdens and Maximum Permissible Concentration of Radionuclides in Air and in Water for Occupational Exposure, NCRP Report Number 22, incorporated by reference in Section 611.102, except the daughter products of thorium-232, uranium-235 and uranium-238.
BOARD NOTE: Derived from 40 CFR 141.2 (1998↑994).

"Maximum contaminant level" ("MCL") means the maximum permissible level of a contaminant in water that is delivered to any user of a public water system. See Section 611.121.
BOARD NOTE: Derived from 40 CFR 141.2 (1998↑994).

"Maximum Total Trihalomethane Potential" or "MTP" means the maximum concentration of total trihalomethanes (TTHMs) produced in a given water containing a disinfectant residual after 7 days at a temperature of 25° C or above.
BOARD NOTE: Derived from 40 CFR 141.2 (1998↑994).

"MFL" means millions of fibers per liter larger than 10 micrometers.
BOARD NOTE: Derived from 40 CFR 141.23(a)(4)(i) (1998↑994).

"mg" means milligrams (1/1000th of a gram).

"mg/L" means milligrams per liter.

"Mixed system" means a PWS that uses both groundwater and surface water sources.
BOARD NOTE: Drawn from 40 CFR 141.23(b)(2) and 141.24(f)(2) note (1998↑994).

"MUG" means 4-methyl-umbelliferyl-beta-d-glucuronide.

"Near the first service connection" means at one of the 20 percent of all service connections in the entire system that are nearest the public water system (PWS) treatment facility, as measured by water transport time within the distribution system.
BOARD NOTE: Derived from 40 CFR 141.2 (1998↑994).

"nm" means nanometer (1/1,000,000,000th of a meter).

"Non-community water system" or "NCWS" or "non-CWS" means a public water system (PWS) that is not a community water system (CWS). A non-community water system is either a "transient non-community water

ILLINOIS REGISTER 2771

POLLUTION CONTROL BOARD

NOTICE OF ADOPTED AMENDMENTS

system (TWS)" or a "non-transient non-community water system (NTNCWS)."
BOARD NOTE: Derived from the definition of "public water system" in 40 CFR 141.2 (1998<del>1994</del>).

"Non-transient non-community water system" or "NTNCWS" means a public water system (PWS) that is not a community water system (CWS) and that regularly serves at least 25 of the same persons over 6 months per year.
BOARD NOTE: Derived from 40 CFR 141.2 (1998<del>1994</del>).

"NPDWR" means "national primary drinking water regulation".

"NTU" means "nephelometric turbidity units".

"Old MCL" means one of the inorganic maximum contaminant levels (MCLs), codified at Section 611.300, or organic MCLs, codified at Section 611.310, including any marked as "additional state requirements."
BOARD NOTE: Old MCLs are those derived prior to the implementation of the U.S. EPA "Phase II" regulations. The Section 611.640 definition of this term, which applies only to Subpart O of this Part, differs from this definition in that the definition does not include the Section 611.300 inorganic MCLs.

"P-A Coliform Test" means "Presence-Absence Coliform Test".

"Performance evaluation sample" means a reference sample provided to a laboratory for the purpose of demonstrating that the laboratory can successfully analyze the sample within limits of performance specified by the Agency; or, for bacteriological laboratories, Public Health; or, for radiological laboratories, the Illinois Department of Nuclear Safety. The true value of the concentration of the reference material is unknown to the laboratory at the time of the analysis.
BOARD NOTE: Derived from 40 CFR 141.2 (1998<del>1994</del>).

"Person" means an individual, corporation, company, association, partnership, State unit of local government, municipality or Federal agency.
BOARD NOTE: Derived from 40 CFR 141.2 (1998<del>1994</del>).

"Phase I" refers to that group of chemical contaminants and the accompanying regulations promulgated by USEPA <del>U.S. EPA</del> on July 8, 1987, at 52 Fed. Reg. 25712.

"Phase II" refers to that group of chemical contaminants and the accompanying regulations promulgated by USEPA <del>U.S. EPA</del> on January 30, 1991, at 56 Fed. Reg. 3578.

ILLINOIS REGISTER 2772

POLLUTION CONTROL BOARD

NOTICE OF ADOPTED AMENDMENTS

"Phase IIB" refers to that group of chemical contaminants and the accompanying regulations promulgated by USEPA <del>U.S. EPA</del> on July 1, 1991, at 56 Fed. Reg. 30266.

"Phase V" refers to that group of chemical contaminants promulgated by USEPA <del>U.S. EPA</del> on July 17, 1992, at 57 Fed. Reg. 31776.

"Picocurie" or "pCi" means the quantity of radioactive material producing 2.22 nuclear transformations per minute.
BOARD NOTE: Derived from 40 CFR 141.2 (1998<del>1994</del>).

"Point of disinfectant application" is the point at which the disinfectant is applied and downstream of which water is not subject to recontamination by surface water runoff.
BOARD NOTE: Derived from 40 CFR 141.2 (1998<del>1994</del>).

"Point-of-entry treatment device" is a treatment device applied to the drinking water entering a house or building for the purpose of reducing contaminants in the drinking water distributed throughout the house or building.
BOARD NOTE: Derived from 40 CFR 141.2 (1998<del>1994</del>).

"Point-of-use treatment device" is a treatment device applied to a single tap used for the purpose of reducing contaminants in drinking water at that one tap.
BOARD NOTE: Derived from 40 CFR 141.2 (1998<del>1994</del>).

"Public Health" means the Illinois Department of Public Health.
BOARD NOTE: The Department of Public Health ("Public Health") regulates non-community water supplies ("non-CWSs", including non-transient, non-community water supplies ("NTNCWSs") and transient non-community water supplies ("transient non-CWSs")). For the purposes of regulation of supplies by Public Health by reference to this Part, "Agency" shall mean Public Health.

"Public water system" or "PWS" means a system for the provision to the public of piped water for human consumption or other constructed conveyances. If such system has at least fifteen service connections or regularly serves an average of at least 25 individuals daily at least 60 days out of the year. A PWS is either a community water system (CWS) or a non-community water system (non-CWS). Such term includes:

Any collection, treatment, storage and distribution facilities under control of the operator of such system and used primarily in connection with such system; and,

Any collection or pretreatment storage facilities not under such

POLLUTION CONTROL BOARD

NOTICE OF ADOPTED AMENDMENTS

control that are used primarily in connection with such system.
BOARD NOTE: Derived from 40 CFR 141.2 (1998+994).

"Reliably and consistently" below a specified level for a contaminant means an Agency determination based on analytical results following the initial detection of a contaminant to determine the qualitative condition of water from an individual sampling point or source. The Agency shall base this determination on the consistency of analytical results, the degree below the MCL, the susceptibility of source water to variation, and other vulnerability factors pertinent to the contaminant detected that may influence the quality of water.
BOARD NOTE: Derived from 40 CFR 141.23(b)(9), 141.24(f)(11)(ii), and 141.24(f)(11)(iii) (1998+994).

"Rem" means the unit of dose equivalent from ionizing radiation to the total body or any internal organ or organ system. A "millirem (mrem)" is 1/1000 of a rem.
BOARD NOTE: Derived from 40 CFR 141.2 (1998+994).

"Repeat compliance period" means a compliance period that begins after the initial compliance period.
BOARD NOTE: Derived from 40 CFR 141.2 (1998+994).

"Representative" means that a sample must reflect the quality of water that is delivered to consumers under conditions when all sources required to supply water under normal conditions are in use and all treatment is properly operating.

"Residual disinfectant concentration" ("RDC" or "C" in CT calculations) means the concentration of disinfectant measured in mg/L in a representative sample of water. For purposes of the requirement of Section 611.241(d) of maintaining a detectable RDC in the distribution system, "RDC" means a residual of free or combined chlorine.
BOARD NOTE: Derived from 40 CFR 141.2 (1998+994).

"Safe Drinking Water Act" or "SDWA" means the Public Health Service Act, as amended by the Safe Drinking Water Act, Pub. L. 93-523, 42 USC W+B+€+ 300f et seq.
BOARD NOTE: Derived from 40 CFR 141.2 (1998+994).

"Sanitary survey" means an onsite review of the water source, facilities, equipment, operation and maintenance of a public water system (PWS) for the purpose of evaluating the adequacy of such source, facilities, equipment, operation and maintenance for producing and distributing safe drinking water.
BOARD NOTE: Derived from 40 CFR 141.2 (1998+994).

POLLUTION CONTROL BOARD

NOTICE OF ADOPTED AMENDMENTS

"Sedimentation" means a process for removal of solids before filtration by gravity or separation.
BOARD NOTE: Derived from 40 CFR 141.2 (1998+994).

"SEP" means special exception permit (Section 611.110).

"Service connection," as used in the definition of public water system, does not include a connection to a system that delivers water by a constructed conveyance other than a pipe if any of the following is true:

The water is used exclusively for purposes other than residential use (consisting of drinking, bathing, and cooking, or other similar uses);

The Agency determines by issuing a SEP that alternative water for residential use or similar uses for drinking and cooking is provided to achieve the equivalent level of public health protection provided by the applicable national primary drinking regulations; or

The Agency determines by issuing a SEP that the water provided for residential use or similar uses for drinking, cooking, and bathing is centrally treated or treated at the point of entry by the provider, a pass-through entity, or the user to achieve the equivalent level of protection provided by the applicable national primary drinking water regulations.
BOARD NOTE: Derived from 40 CFR 141.2 (1998). See sections 1401(4)(B)(i)(II) and (4)(B)(i)(III) of SDWA (42 USC 300f(4)(B)(i)(II) and (4)(B)(i)(III) (1996)).

"Slow sand filtration" means a process involving passage of raw water through a bed of sand at low velocity (generally less than 0.4 meters per hour (m/h)) resulting in substantial particulate removal by physical and biological mechanisms.
BOARD NOTE: Derived from 40 CFR 141.2 (1998+994).

"SOC" or "Synthetic organic chemical contaminant" refers to that group of contaminants designated as "SOCs", or "synthetic organic chemicals" or "synthetic organic contaminants", in U.S. EPA regulatory discussions and guidance documents. "SOCs" include alachlor, aldicarb, aldicarb sulfone, aldicarb sulfoxide, atrazine, benzo(a)pyrene, carbofuran, chlordane, dalapon, dibromoethylene (ethylene dibromide or EDB), dibromochloropropane (DBCP), di(2-ethylhexyl)adipate, di(2-ethylhexyl)phthalate, dinoseb, diquat, endothall, endrin, glyphosate, heptachlor, heptachlor epoxide, hexachlorobenzene, hexachlorocyclopentadiene, lindane, methoxychlor, oxamyl, pentachlorophenol, picloram, simazine, toxaphene,

ILLINOIS REGISTER 2775

POLLUTION CONTROL BOARD

NOTICE OF ADOPTED AMENDMENTS

polychlorinated biphenyls (PCBs), 2,4-D, 2,3,7,8-TCDD, and 2,4,5-TP.

"Source" means a well, reservoir, or other source of raw water.

"Special irrigation district" means an irrigation district in existence prior to May 18, 1994 that provides primarily agricultural service through a piped water system with only incidental residential use or similar use, where the system or the residential users or similar users of the system comply with either of the following exclusion conditions:

    The Agency determines by issuing a SEP that alternative water is provided for residential use or similar uses for drinking or cooking to achieve the equivalent level of public health protection provided by the applicable national primary drinking water regulations; or

    The Agency determines by issuing a SEP that the water provided for residential use or similar uses for drinking, cooking, and bathing is centrally treated or treated at the point of entry by the provider, a pass-through entity, or the user to achieve the equivalent level of protection provided by the applicable national primary drinking water regulations.
BOARD NOTE: Derived from 40 CFR 141.2 (1998) and sections 1401(4)(B)(i)(II) and (4)(B)(i)(III) of SDWA (42 USC 300f(4)(B)(i)(II) and (4)(B)(i)(III) (1996)).

"Standard sample" means the aliquot of finished drinking water that is examined for the presence of coliform bacteria.
BOARD NOTE: Derived from 40 CFR 141.2 (1998 1994).

"Supplier of water" or "supplier" means any person who owns or operates a public water system (PWS). This term includes the "official custodian".
BOARD NOTE: Derived from 40 CFR 141.2 (1998 1994).

"Surface water" means all water that is open to the atmosphere and subject to surface runoff.
BOARD NOTE: Derived from 40 CFR 141.2 (1998 1994).

"SWS" means "surface water system", a public water supply (PWS) that uses only surface water sources, including "groundwater under the direct influence of surface water".
BOARD NOTE: Drawn from 40 CFR 141.23(b)(2) and 141.24(f)(2) note (1998 1994).

"System with a single service connection" means a system that supplies drinking water to consumers via a single service line.

ILLINOIS REGISTER 2776

POLLUTION CONTROL BOARD

NOTICE OF ADOPTED AMENDMENTS

BOARD NOTE: Derived from 40 CFR 141.2 (1998 1994).

"Too numerous to count" means that the total number of bacterial colonies exceeds 200 on a 47-mm diameter membrane filter used for coliform detection.
BOARD NOTE: Derived from 40 CFR 141.2 (1998 1994).

"Total trihalomethanes" or "TTHM" means the sum of the concentration of trihalomethanes (THMs), in milligrams per liter (mg/L), rounded to two significant figures.
BOARD NOTE: Derived from the definition of "total trihalomethanes" in 40 CFR 141.2 (1998 1994). See the definition of TTHMs for a listing of the four compounds that USEPA U.S. EPA considers TTHMs to comprise.

"Transient, non-community water system" or "transient non-CWS" means a non-CWS that does not regularly serve at least 25 of the same persons over six months of the year.
BOARD NOTE: Derived from 40 CFR 141.2 (1998 1994). The federal regulations apply to all "public water systems", which are defined as all systems having at least 15 service connections or regularly serving water to at least 25 persons. See 43 USC U.S.C. 300f(4). The Act mandates that the Board and the Agency regulate "public water supplies", which it defines as having at least 15 service connections or regularly serving 25 persons daily at least 60 days per year. See Section 3.28 of the Act [415 ILCS 5/3.28]. The Department of Public Health regulates transient non-community water systems.

"Treatment" means any process that changes the physical, chemical, microbiological, or radiological properties of water, is under the control of the supplier, and is not a "point of use" or "point of entry treatment device" as defined in this Section. "Treatment" includes, but is not limited to aeration, coagulation, sedimentation, filtration, activated carbon treatment, disinfection, and fluoridation.

"Trihalomethane" or "THM" means one of the family of organic compounds, named as derivatives of methane, wherein three of the four hydrogen atoms in methane are each substituted by a halogen atom in the molecular structure. The THM are:
    Trichloromethane (coliform),
    Dibromochloromethane,
    Bromodichloromethane and
    Tribromomethane (bromoform).
BOARD NOTE: Derived from the definitions of "total trihalomethanes" and "trihalomethanes" in 40 CFR 141.2 (1998 1994).

"ug" means micrograms (1/1,000,000th of a gram).

ILLINOIS REGISTER 2777
99

POLLUTION CONTROL BOARD

NOTICE OF ADOPTED AMENDMENTS

"USEPA or U.S. EPA" means the U.S. Environmental Protection Agency.

"Virus" means a virus of fecal origin that is infectious to humans by waterborne transmission.

"VOC" or "volatile organic chemical contaminant" refers to that group of contaminants designated as VOCs", or "volatile organic chemicals" or "volatile organic contaminants", in USEPA B+θ+-EPA regulatory discussions and guidance documents. "VOCs" include benzene, dichloromethane, tetrachloromethane (carbon tetrachloride), trichloroethylene, vinyl chloride, 1,1,1-trichloroethane (methyl chloroform), 1,1-dichloroethane, 1,2 dichloroethane, cis-1,2-dichloroethylene, ethylbenzene, monochlorobenzene, o-dichloro-benzene, styrene, 1,2,4-trichlorobenzene, 1,1,2-trichloroethane, tetrachloroethylene, toluene, trans-1,2-dichloroethylene, xylene, and 1,2-dichloropropane.
BOARD NOTE: Derived from 40 CFR 141.2 (1998⟨⟩1994).

"Waterborne disease outbreak" means the significant occurrence of acute infectious illness, epidemiologically associated with the ingestion of water from a public water system (PWS) that is deficient in treatment, as determined by the appropriate local or State agency.
BOARD NOTE: Derived from 40 CFR 141.2 (1998⟨⟩1994).

"Wellhead Protection Program" means the wellhead protection program for the State of Illinois, approved by USEPA U+S+-EPA under section 1428 of the SDWA.
BOARD NOTE: Derived from 40 CFR 141.71(b) (1998⟨⟩1994). The wellhead protection program will include the "groundwater protection needs assessment" under Section 17.1 of the Act, and regulations to be adopted in 35 Ill. Adm. Code 615 et seq.

(Source: Amended at 23 Ill. Reg. 2756, effective FEB 17 1999)

Section 611.102 Incorporations by Reference

a) Abbreviations and short-name listing of references. The following names and abbreviated names, presented in alphabetical order, are used in this Part to refer to materials incorporated by reference:

"Amco-AEPA-1 Polymer" is available from Advanced Polymer Systems.

"ASTM Method" means a method published by and available from the American Society for Testing and Materials (ASTM).

"Colisure Test" means "Colisure Presence/Absence Test for Detection and Identification of Coliform Bacteria and Escherichia

ILLINOIS REGISTER 2778
99

POLLUTION CONTROL BOARD

NOTICE OF ADOPTED AMENDMENTS

Coli in Drinking Water", available from Millipore Corporation, Technical Services Department.

"Dioxin and Furan Method 1613" means "Tetra- through Octa-Chlorinated Dioxins and Furans by Isotope-Dilution HRGC/HRMS", available from NTIS.

"GLI Method 2" means GLI Method 2, "Turbidity", Nov. 2, 1992, available from Great Lakes Instruments, Inc.

"Guidance Manual for Compliance with the Filtration and Disinfection Requirements for Public Water Systems Using Surface Water Sources", available from USEPA Science and Technology Branch.

"BASL Procedure Manual" means BASL Procedure Manual, BASL 300, available from ERDA Health and Safety Laboratory.

"Maximum Permissible Body Burdens and Maximum Permissible Concentrations of Radionuclides in Air and in Water for Occupational Exposure", NCRP Report Number 22, available from NCRP.

"NCRP" means "National Council on Radiation Protection".

"NTIS" means "National Technical Information Service".

"New Jersey Radium Method" means "Determination of Radium 228 in Drinking Water", available from the New Jersey Department of Environmental Protection.

"New York Radium Method" means "Determination of Ra-226 and Ra-228 (Ra-02)", available from the New York Department of Public Health.

"OMGP-MUG Test" (meaning "minimal medium ortho-nitrophenyl-beta-d-galactopyranoside-4-methyl-umbelliferyl-beta-d-glucuronide test"), also called the "Autoanalysis Colilert System", is Method 9223, available in "Standard Methods for the Examination of Water and Wastewater", 18th ed., from American Public Health Association.

"Procedures for Radiochemical Analysis of Nuclear Reactor Aqueous Solutions", available from NTIS.

"Radiochemical Methods" means "Interim Radiochemical Methodology for Drinking Water", available from NTIS.

ILLINOIS REGISTER 2779

POLLUTION CONTROL BOARD

NOTICE OF ADOPTED AMENDMENTS

"Standard Methods", means "Standard Methods for the Examination of Water and Wastewater", available from the American Public Health Association or the American Waterworks Association.

"Technical Bulletin 601" means "Technical Bulletin 601, Standard Method of Testing for Nitrate in Drinking Water", July, 1994, available from Analytical Technology, Inc.

"Technicon Methods" means "Fluoride in Water and Wastewater", available from Technicon.

"USDOE Manual" means "EML Procedures Manual", available from the United State Department of Energy.

"USEPA Asbestos Methods - 100.1" means Method 100.1, "Analytical Method for Determination of Asbestos Fibers in Water", available from NTIS.

"USEPA Asbestos Methods-100.2" means Method 100.2, "Determination of Asbestos Structures over 10-um in Length in Drinking Water", available from NTIS.

"USEPA Environmental Inorganics Methods" means "Methods for the Determination of Inorganic Substances in Environmental Samples", available from NTIS.

"USEPA Environmental Metals Methods" means "Methods for the Determination of Metals in Environmental Samples", available from NTIS.

"USEPA Organic Methods" means "Methods for the Determination of Organic Compounds in Drinking Water", July, 1991, for Methods 502.2, 505, 507, 508, 508A, 515.1, and 531.1; "Methods for the Determination of Organic Compounds in Drinking Water--Supplement I", July, 1990, for Methods 506, 547, 550, 550.L, and 551; and "Methods for the Determination of Organic Compounds in Drinking Water--Supplement II", August, 1992, for Methods 515.2, 524.2, 548.1, 549.1, 552.1, and 555, available from NTIS. Methods 504.I, 508.I, and 525.2 are available from EPA EMSL.

"USGS Methods" means "Methods of Analysis by the U.S. Geological Survey National Water Quality Laboratory--Determination of Inorganic and Organic Constituents in Water and Fluvial Sediments", available from NTIS and USGS.

"USEPA Interim Radiochemical Methods" means "Interim Radiochemical Methodology for Drinking Water", EPA 600/4-75-008 (revised), March 1976. Available from NTIS.

ILLINOIS REGISTER 2780

POLLUTION CONTROL BOARD

NOTICE OF ADOPTED AMENDMENTS

"USEPA Radioactivity Methods" means "Prescribed Procedures for Measurement of Radioactivity in Drinking Water", EPA 600/4-80-032, August 1980. Available from NTIS.

"USEPA Radiochemical Analyses" means "Radiochemical Analytical Procedures for Analysis of Environmental Samples", March 1979. Available from NTIS.

"USEPA Radiochemistry Methods" means "Radiochemistry Procedures Manual", EPA 520/5-84-006, December 1987. Available from NTIS.

"USEPA Technical Notes" means "Technical Notes on Drinking Water Methods", available from NTIS.

"Waters Method B-1011" means "Waters Test Method for the Determination of Nitrite/Nitrate in Water Using Single Column Ion Chromatography", available from Millipore Corporation, Waters Chromatography Division.

b) The Board incorporates the following publications by reference:

Access Analytical Systems, Inc., See Environetics, Inc.

Advanced Polymer Systems, 3696 Haven Avenue, Redwood City, CA 94063 415-366-2626:

Amco-AEPA-1 Polymer. See 40 CFR 141.22(a) (1995). Also, as referenced in ASTM D1889.

American Public Health Association, 1015 Fifteenth Street NW, Washington, DC 20005 800-645-5476:

"Standard Methods for the Examination of Water and Wastewater", 17th Edition 1989 (referred to as "Standard Methods, 17th ed.").

"Standard Methods for the Examination of Water and Wastewater", 18th Edition, 1992, including "Supplement to the 18th Edition of Standard Methods for the Examination of Water and Wastewater", 1994 (collectively referred to as "Standard Methods, 18th ed."). See the methods listed separately for the same references under American Water Works Association.

"Standard Methods for the Examination of Water and Wastewater", 19th Edition, 1995 (referred to as "Standard Methods, 19th ed.").

ILLINOIS REGISTER

POLLUTION CONTROL BOARD

NOTICE OF ADOPTED AMENDMENTS

American Waterworks Association et al., 6666 West Quincy Ave., Denver, CO 80235 303-794-7711;

Standard Methods for the Examination of Water and Wastewater, 13th Edition, 1971 (referred to as "Standard Methods, 13th ed.").

Method 302, Gross Alpha and Gross Beta Radioactivity in Water (Total, Suspended and Dissolved).

Method 303, Total Radioactive Strontium and Strontium 90 in Water.

Method 304, Radium in Water by Precipitation.

Method 305, Radium 226 by Radon in Water (Soluble, Suspended and Total).

Method 306, Tritium in Water.

Standard Methods for the Examination of Water and Wastewater, 18th Edition, 1992 (referred to as "Standard Methods, 18th ed."):

Method 2130 B, Turbidity, Nephelometric Method.

Method 2320 B, Alkalinity, Titration Method.

Method 2510 B, Conductivity, Laboratory Method.

Method 2550, Temperature, Laboratory and Field Methods.

Method 3111 B, Metals by Flame Atomic Absorption Spectrometry, Direct Air-Acetylene Flame Method.

Method 3111 D, Metals by Flame Atomic Absorption Spectrometry, Direct Nitrous Oxide-Acetylene Flame Method.

Method 3112 B, Metals by Cold-Vapor Atomic Absorption Spectrometry, Cold-Vapor Atomic Absorption Spectrometric Method.

Method 3113 B, Metals by Electrothermal Atomic Absorption Spectrometry, Electrothermal Atomic Absorption Spectrometric Method.

POLLUTION CONTROL BOARD

NOTICE OF ADOPTED AMENDMENTS

Method 3114 B, Metals by Hydride Generation/Atomic Absorption Spectrometry, Manual Hydride Generation/Atomic Absorption Spectrometric Method.

Method 3120 B, Metals by Plasma Emission Spectroscopy, Inductively Coupled Plasma (ICP) Method.

Method 3500-Ca D, Calcium, EDTA Titrimetric Method.

Method 4110 B, Determination of Anions by Ion Chromatography, Ion Chromatography with Chemical Suppression of Eluent Conductivity.

Method 4500-CN(-) C, Cyanide, Total Cyanide after Distillation.

Method 4500-CN(-) E, Cyanide, Colorimetric Method.

Method 4500-CN(-) F, Cyanide, Cyanide-Selective Electrode Method.

Method 4500-CN(-) G, Cyanide, Cyanides Amenable to Chlorination after Distillation.

Method 4500-Cl D, Chlorine (Residual), Amperometric Titration Method.

Method 4500-Cl E, Chlorine (Residual), Low-Level Amperometric Titration Method.

Method 4500-Cl F, Chlorine (Residual), DPD Ferrous Titrimetric Method.

Method 4500-Cl G, Chlorine (Residual), DPD Colorimetric Method.

Method 4500-Cl H, Chlorine (Residual), Syringaldazine (FACTS) Method.

Method 4500-Cl I, Chlorine (Residual), Iodometric Electrode Technique.

Method 4500-ClO(2) C, Chlorine Dioxide, Amperometric Method I.

Method 4500-ClO(2) D, Chlorine Dioxide, DPD Method.

Method 4500-ClO(2) E, Chlorine Dioxide, Amperometric

ILLINOIS REGISTER 2783

POLLUTION CONTROL BOARD

NOTICE OF ADOPTED AMENDMENTS

Method II (Proposed).

Method 4500-F(-) B, Fluoride, Preliminary Distillation Step.

Method 4500-F(-) C, Fluoride, Ion-Selective Electrode Method.

Method 4500-F(-) D, Fluoride, SPADNS Method.

Method 4500-F(-) E, Fluoride, Complexone Method.

Method 4500-H(+) B, pH Value, Electrometric Method.

Method 4500-NO[2](-) B, Nitrogen (Nitrite), Colorimetric Method.

Method 4500-NO[3](-) D, Nitrogen (Nitrate), Nitrate Electrode Method.

Method 4500-NO[3](-) E, Nitrogen (Nitrate), Cadmium Reduction Method.

Method 4500-NO[3](-) F, Nitrogen (Nitrate), Automated Cadmium Reduction Method.

Method 4500-O[3] B, Ozone (Residual) (Proposed), Indigo Colorimetric Method.

Method 4500-P E, Phosphorus, Ascorbic Acid Method.

Method 4500-P F, Phosphorus, Automated Ascorbic Acid Reduction Method.

Method 4500-Si D, Silica, Molybdosilicate Method.

Method 4500-Si E, Silica, Heteropoly Blue Method.

Method 4500-Si F, Silica, Automated Method for Molybdate-Reactive Silica.

Method 4500-SO[4](2-) C, Sulfate, Gravimetric Method with Ignition of Residue.

Method 4500-SO[4](2-) D, Sulfate, Gravimetric Method with Drying of Residue.

Method 4500-SO[4](2-) F, Sulfate, Automated

ILLINOIS REGISTER 2784

POLLUTION CONTROL BOARD

NOTICE OF ADOPTED AMENDMENTS

Methylthymol Blue Method.

method 6610, Carbamate Pesticide Method.

Method 6651, Glyphosate Herbicide (Proposed).

Method 7110 B, Gross Alpha and Beta Radioactivity (Total, Suspended, and Dissolved), Evaporation Method for Gross Alpha-Beta.

Method 7110 C, Gross Alpha and Beta Radioactivity (Total, Suspended, and Dissolved), Coprecipitation Method for Gross Alpha Radioactivity in Drinking Water (Proposed).

Method 7500-Cs B, Radioactive Cesium, Precipitation Method.

Method 7500-3H, B, Tritium, Liquid Scintillation Spectrometric Method

Method 7500-I B, Radioactive Iodine, Precipitation Method.

Method 7500-I C, Radioactive Iodine, Ion-Exchange Method.

Method 7500-I D, Radioactive Iodine, Distillation Method.

Method 7500-Ra B, Radium, Precipitation Method.

Method 7500-Ra C, Radium, Emanation Method.

Method 7500-Ra D, Radium, Sequential Precipitation Method (Proposed).

Method 7500-U B, Uranium, Radiochemical Method (Proposed).

Method 7500-U C, Uranium, Isotopic Method (Proposed).

Method 9215 B, Heterotrophic Plate Count, Pour Plate Method.

Method 9221 A, Multiple-Tube Fermentation Technique for Members of the Coliform Group, Introduction.

POLLUTION CONTROL BOARD

NOTICE OF ADOPTED AMENDMENTS

Method 9221 B, Multiple-Tube Fermentation Technique for Members of the Coliform Group, Standard Total Coliform Fermentation Technique.

Method 9221 C, Multiple-Tube Fermentation Technique for Members of the Coliform Group, Estimation of Bacterial Density.

Method 9221 D, Multiple-Tube Fermentation Technique for Members of the Coliform Group, Presence-Absence (P-A) Coliform Test.

Method 9222 A, Membrane Filter Technique for Members of the Coliform Group, Introduction.

Method 9222 B, Membrane Filter Technique for Members of the Coliform Group, Standard Total Coliform Membrane Filter Procedure.

Method 9222 C, Membrane Filter Technique for Members of the Coliform Group, Delayed-Incubation Total Coliform Procedure.

Method 9223, Chromogenic Substrate Coliform Test (Preposed).

~~Standard Methods for the Examination of Water and Wastewater-18th Edition-Supplement-1994 (Referred to as "Standard Methods, 18th ed.");~~

Standard Methods for the Examination of Water and Wastewater, 19th Edition, 1995 (referred to as "Standard Methods, 19th ed."):

Method 7120-B, Gamma Spectrometric Method.

Method 7500-U C, Uranium, Isotopic Method.

Analytical Technology, Inc. ATI Orion, 529 Main Street, Boston, MA 02129;

Technical Bulletin 601, "Standard Method of Testing for Nitrate in Drinking Water", July, 1994, PN 221890-001 (referred to as "Technical Bulletin 601").

ASTM. American Society for Testing and Materials, 1976 Race Street, Philadelphia, PA 19103 215-299-5585;

POLLUTION CONTROL BOARD

NOTICE OF ADOPTED AMENDMENTS

ASTM Method D511-93 A and B, "Standard Test Methods for Calcium and Magnesium in Water", "Test Method A--complexometric Titration" & "Test Method B--Atomic Absorption Spectrophotometric", approved 1993.

ASTM Method D515-88 A, "Standard Test Methods for Phosphorus in Water", "Test Method A--Colorimetric Ascorbic Acid Reduction", approved August 19, 1988.

ASTM Method D859-88, "Standard Test Method for Silica in Water", approved August 19, 1988.

ASTM Method D1067-92 B, "Standard Test Methods for Acidity or Alkalinity in Water", "Test Method B--Electrometric or Color-Change Titration", approved May 15, 1992.

ASTM Method D1125-91 A, "Standard Test Methods for Electrical Conductivity and Resistivity of Water", "Test Method A--Field and Routine Laboratory Measurement of Static (Non-Flowing) Samples", approved June 15, 1991.

ASTM Method D1179-93 B "Standard Test Methods for Fluoride in Water", "Test Method B--Ion Selective Electrode", approved 1993.

ASTM Method D1293-84 "Standard Test Methods for pH of Water", "Test Method A--Precise Laboratory Measurement" & "Test Method B--Routine or Continuous Measurement", approved October 26, 1984.

ASTM Method D1688-90 A or C, "Standard Test Methods for Copper in Water", "Test Method A--Atomic Absorption, Direct" & "Test Method C--Atomic Absorbtion, Graphite Furnace", approved March 15, 1990.

ASTM Method D2036-91 A or B, "Standard Test Methods for Cyanide in Water", "Test Method A--Total Cyanides after Distillation" & "Test Method B--Cyanides Amenable to Chlorination by Difference", approved September 15, 1991.

ASTM Method D2459-72, "Standard Test Method for Gamma Spectrometry in Water", approved July 28, 1973, discontinued in 1988.

ASTM Method D2460-90, "Standard Test Method for Radionuclides of Radium in Water", approved 1990.

ASTM Method D2907-91, "Standard Test Methods for

POLLUTION CONTROL BOARD

NOTICE OF ADOPTED AMENDMENTS

Microquantities of Uranium in Water by Fluorometry", "Test Method A--Direct Fluorometric" & "Test Method B--Extraction", approved June 15, 1991.

ASTM Method D2972-93 B or C, "Standard Test Methods for Arsenic in Water", "Test Method B--Atomic Absorption, Hydride Generation" & "Test Method C--Atomic Absorption, Graphite Furnace", approved 1993.

ASTM Method D3223-91, "Standard Test Method for Total Mercury in Water", approved September 23, 1991.

ASTM Method D3454-91, "Standard Test Method for Radium-226 in Water", approved 1991.

ASTM Method D3559-90 D, "Standard Test Methods for Lead in Water", "Test Method D--Atomic Absorption, Graphite Furnace", approved August 6, 1990.

ASTM Method D3645-93 B, "Standard Test Methods for Beryllium in Water", "Method B--Atomic Absorption, Graphite Furnace", approved 1993.

ASTM Method D3649-91, "Standard Test Method for High-Resolution Gamma-Ray Spectrometry of Water", approved 1991.

ASTM Method D2697-02, "Standard Test Method for Antimony in Water", approved June 15, 1992.

ASTM Method D3859-93 A, "Standard Test Methods for Selenium in Water", "Method A--Atomic Absorption, Hydride Method", approved 1993.

ASTM Method D3867-90 A and B, "Standard Test Methods for Nitrite-Nitrate in Water", "Test Method A--Automated Cadmium Reduction" & "Test Method B--Manual Cadmium Reduction", approved January 10, 1990.

ASTM Method D3972-90, "Standard Test Method for Isotopic Uranium in Water by Radiochemistry", approved 1990.

ASTM Method D4107-91, "Standard Test Method for Tritium in Drinking Water", approved 1991.

ASTM Method D4327-91, "Standard Test Method for Anions in Water by Ion Chromatography", approved October 15, 1991.

POLLUTION CONTROL BOARD

NOTICE OF ADOPTED AMENDMENTS

ASTM Method D4785-88, "Standard Test Method for Low-Level Iodine-131 in Water", approved 1988.

ASTM Method D5174-91, "Standard Test Method for Trace Uranium in Water by Pulsed-Laser Phosphorimetry", approved 1991.

ERDA Health and Safety Laboratory, New York, NY:

HASL Procedure Manual, HASL 300, 1973. See 40 CFR 141.25(b)(2) (1995).

Great Lakes Instruments, Inc., 8855 North 55th Street, Milwaukee, WI 53223:

GLI Method 2, "Turbidity", Nov. 2, 1992.

Millipore Corporation, Technical Services Department, 80 Ashby Road, Milford, MA 01730 800-654-5476:

Colisure Presence/Absence Test for Detection and Identification of Coliform Bacteria and Escherichia Coli in Drinking Water, February 28, 1994 (referred to as "Colisure Test").

Millipore Corporation, Waters Chromatography Division, 34 Maple St., Milford, MA 01757 800-252-4752:

Waters Test Method for the Determination of Nitrite/Nitrate in Water Using Single Column Ion Chromatography, Method B-1011 (referred to as "Waters Method B-1011").

NCRP. National Council on Radiation Protection, 7910 Woodmont Ave., Bethesda, MD 301-657-2652:

"Maximum Permissible Body Burdens and Maximum Permissible Concentrations of Radionuclides in Air and in Water for Occupational Exposure", NCRP Report Number 22, June 5, 1959.

NSF. National Sanitation Foundation International, 3475 Plymouth Road, PO Box 130140, Ann Arbor, Michigan 48113-0140 (telephone: 734-769-8010):

NSF Standard 61, section 9, September 1994.

NTIS. National Technical Information Service, U.S. Department of Commerce, 5285 Port Royal Road, Springfield, VA 22161 (703) 487-4600 or (800) 553-6847:

POLLUTION CONTROL BOARD

NOTICE OF ADOPTED AMENDMENTS

"Interim Radiochemical Methodology for Drinking Water", EPA 600/4-75-008 (revised), March 1976 (referred to as "USEPA Interim Radiochemical Methods"). (Pages 1, 4, 6, 9, 13, 16, 24, 29, 34)

Method 100.1, "Analytical Method for Determination of Asbestos Fibers in Water", EPA-600/4-83-043, September, 1983, Doc. No. PB83-260471 (referred to as "USEPA Asbestos Methods-100.1").

Method 100.2, "Determination of Asbestos Structures over 10-mm in Length in Drinking Water", EPA-600/4-83-043, June, 1994, Doc. No. PB94-201902 (Referred to as "USEPA Asbestos Methods-100.2").

"Methods for Chemical Analysis of Water and Wastes", March, 1983, Doc. No. PB84-128677 (referred to as "USEPA Inorganic Methods"). (Methods 150.1, 150.2, and 245.2, which formerly appeared in this reference, are available from USEPA EMSL.)

"Methods for the Determination of Metals in Environmental Samples", June, 1991, Doc. No. PB91-231498 (referred to as "USEPA Environmental Metals Methods").

"Methods for the Determination of Organic Compounds in Drinking Water", December, 1988, revised July, 1991, EPA-600/4-88/039 (referred to as "USEPA Organic Methods"). (For methods 502.2, 505, 507, 508, 508A, 515.1 and 531.1.)

"Methods for the Determination of Organic Compounds in Drinking Water--Supplement I", July, 1990, EPA-600-4-90-020 (referred to as "USEPA Organic Methods"). (For methods 506, 547, 550, 550.1, and 551.)

"Methods for the Determination of Organic Compounds in Drinking Water--Supplement II", August, 1992, EPA-600/R-92-129 (referred to as "USEPA Organic Methods"). (For methods 515.2, 524.2, 548.1, 549.1, 552.1 and 555.)

"Prescribed Procedures for Measurement of Radioactivity in Drinking Water", EPA 600/4-80-032, August 1980 (referred to as "USEPA Radioactivity Methods"). (Methods 900, 901, 901.1, 902, 903, 903.1, 904, 905, 906, 908, 908.1)

"Procedures for Radiochemical Analysis of Nuclear Reactor Aqueous Solutions", H.L. Krieger and S. Gold, EPA-R4-73-014, May, 1973, Doc. No. PB222-154/7BA.

POLLUTION CONTROL BOARD

NOTICE OF ADOPTED AMENDMENTS

"Radiochemical Analytical Procedures for Analysis of Environmental Samples", March, 1979, Doc. No. EM6LLV 053917 (referred to as "USEPA Radiochemical Analyses"). (Pages 1, 19, 33, 65, 87, 92)

"Radiochemistry Procedures Manual", EPA-520/5-84-006, December, 1987, Doc. No. PB-84-215581 (referred to as "USEPA Radiochemistry Methods"). (Methods 00-01, 00-02, 00-07, H-02, Ra-03, Ra-04, Ra-05, Sr-04)

"Technical Notes on Drinking Water Methods", EPA-600/R-94-173, October, 1994, Doc. No. PB-104766 (referred to as "OSEPA Technical Notes").
BOARD NOTE: USEPA made the following assertion with regard to this reference at 40 CFR 141.23(k)(1) and 141.24(e) and (n)(11) (1995): "This document contains other analytical test procedures and approved analytical methods that remain available for compliance monitoring until July 1, 1996."

"Tetra- through Octa-Chlorinated Dioxins and Furans by Isotope Dilution HRGC/HRMS", October, 1994, EPA-821-B-94-005 (referred to as "Dioxin and Furan Method 1613").

New Jersey Department of Environment, Division of Environmental Quality, Bureau of Radiation and Inorganic Analytical Services, 9 Ewing Street, Trenton, NJ 08625:

"Determination of Radium 228 in Drinking Water", August 1980.

New York Department of Health, Radiological Sciences Institute, Center for Laboratories and Research, Empire State Plaza, Albany, NY 12201:

"Determination of Ra-226 and Ra-228 (Ra-02)", January 1980, revised June 1982.

Technicon Industrial Systems, Tarrytown, NY 10591:

"Fluoride in Water and Wastewater", Industrial Method #129-71W, December, 1972 (referred to as "Technicon Methods: Method #129-71W"). See 40 CFR 141.23(k)(1), footnote 11 (1995).

"Fluoride in Water and Wastewater, #380-75WE, February, 1976 (referred to as "Technicon Methods: Method #380-75WE"). See 40 CFR 141.23(k)(1), footnote 11 (1995).

ILLINOIS REGISTER 2791
99

POLLUTION CONTROL BOARD

NOTICE OF ADOPTED AMENDMENTS

United States Department of Energy, available at the Environmental Measurements Laboratory, U.S. Department of Energy, 376 Hudson Street, New York, NY 10014-3621:

"EML Procedures Manual", 27th Edition, Volume 1, 1990.

United States Environmental Protection Agency, EMSL, Cincinnati, OH 45268 513-569-7586:

"Interim Radiochemical Methodology for Drinking Water", EPA-600/4-75-008 (referred to as "Radiochemical Methods"), (Revised) March, 1976.

"Methods for the Determination of Organic Compounds in Finished Drinking Water and Raw Source Water" (referred to as "USEPA Organic Methods"). (For methods 504.1, 508.1, and 525.2 only.) See NTIS.

"Procedures for Radiochemical Analysis of Nuclear Reactor Aqueous Solutions". See NTIS.

USEPA, Science and Technology Branch, Criteria and Standards Division, Office of Drinking Water, Washington D.C. 20460:

"Guidance Manual for Compliance with the Filtration and Disinfection Requirements for Public Water Systems using Surface Water Sources", October, 1989.

USGS Books and Open-File Reports Section, United States Geological Survey, Federal Center, Box 25425, Denver, CO 80225-0425:

Methods available upon request by method number from "Methods of Analysis by the U.S. Geological Survey National Water Quality Laboratory—Determination of Inorganic and Organic Constituents in Water and Fluvial Sediments", Open File Report 93-125 or Book 5, Chapter A-1, "Methods for Determination of Inorganic Substances in Water and Fluvial Sediments", 3d ed., open-File Report 85-495, 1989, as appropriate (referred to as "USGS Methods").

I-1030-85

I-1062-85

I-1601-85

I-1700-85

ILLINOIS REGISTER 2792
99

POLLUTION CONTROL BOARD

NOTICE OF ADOPTED AMENDMENTS

I-2598-85

I-2601-90

I-2700-85

I-3300-85

Methods available upon request by method number from "Methods for Determination of Radioactive Substances in Water and Fluvial Sediments", Chapter A5 in Book 5 of "Techniques of Water-Resources Investigations of the United States Geological Survey", 1997.

R-1110-76

R-1111-76

R-1120-76

R-1140-76

R-1141-76

R-1142-76

R-1160-76

R-1171-76

R-1180-76

R-1181-76

R-1182-76

o) The Board incorporates the following federal regulations by reference: 40 CFR 136, Appendix B and C (1998+995):

d) This Part incorporates no later amendments or editions.

(Source: Amended at 23 Ill. Reg. 2Y5ᵦ , effective FEB 17 1999)

Section 611.126 Prohibition on Use of Lead

a) In general. Prohibition. Any pipe, any pipe or plumbing fitting or fixture, solder or fluxy shall be lead free, as defined by subsection (b) (d), if it is used after June 19, 1986+ in the installation or

ILLINOIS REGISTER 2793
99

POLLUTION CONTROL BOARD

NOTICE OF ADOPTED AMENDMENTS

repair of:
1) Any PWS;; or
2) Any plumbing in a residential or nonresidential facility providing water for human consumption that which is connected to a PWS. This subsection (a) does not apply to leaded joints necessary for the repair of cast iron pipes.
b)d) Definition of lead free. For purposes of this Section, the term "lead free":
1) When used with respect to solders and flux, refers to solders and flux containing not more than 0.2 percent lead;; and
2) When used with respect to pipes and pipe fittings, refers to pipes and pipe fittings containing not more than 8.0 percent lead; and ⁻
3) when used with respect to plumbing fittings and fixtures, refers to plumbing fittings and fixtures in compliance with NSF Standard 61, section 9, incorporated by reference in Section 611.102.
BOARD NOTE: Derived from 40 CFR 141.43 (a) and (d) (1998⁻1989) and 42 USC 300g-6(a)(1) (1998).

(Source: Amended at 23 Ill. Reg. 2756, effective FEB 17 99 .)

SUBPART C: USE OF NON-CENTRALIZED TREATMENT DEVICES

Section 611.290 Use of Point-of-Use Devices or Bottled Water

a) Suppliers shall not use bottled water or point-of-use devices to achieve compliance with an MCL.
b) Bottled water or point-of-use devices may be used on a temporary basis to avoid an unreasonable risk to health pursuant to a SEP granted by the Agency under Section 611.110.
c) Any use of bottled water must comply with the substantive requirements of Section 611.130(e), except that the supplier shall submit its quality control plan for Agency review as part of its SEP request, rather than for Board review.
BOARD NOTE: Derived from 40 CFR 141.101 (1998⁻1992).

(Source: Amended at 23 Ill. Reg. 2755, effective FEB 17 99 .)

ILLINOIS REGISTER 2794
99

POLLUTION CONTROL BOARD

NOTICE OF ADOPTED AMENDMENTS

1) Heading of the Part: Standards for New Solid Waste Landfills

2) Code Citation: 35 Ill. Adm. Code 811

3) Section Numbers: Adopted Action:
   811.706   Amended
   811.707   Amended
   811.719   Added
   811.720   Added
   811.Appendix B   Amended

4) Statutory Authority: 415 ILCS 5/22.40 and 27

5) Effective date of amendments: February 17, 1999

6) Does this rulemaking contain an automatic repeal date? No

7) Do these amendments contain incorporations by reference? No

8) The adopted amendments, a copy of the Board's opinion and order adopted February 4, 1999, and all materials incorporated by reference are on file at the Board's principal office and are available for public inspection and copying.

9) Notice of proposal published in Illinois Register: December 11, 1998, 22 Ill. Reg. 21276

10) Has JCAR issued a Statement of Objections to these amendments? No. Section 22.40(a) of the Environmental Protection Act [415 ILCS 5/22.40(a)] provides that Section 5 of the Administrative Procedure Act [5 ILCS 100/5-35 and 5-40] shall not apply. Because this rulemaking is not subject to Section 5 of the APA, it is not subject to first notice or to second notice review by JCAR.

11) Differences between proposal and final version: The Board did not make significant changes in the text of the proposed amendments. We did, however, make a number of minor changes at the suggestion of JCAR or on our own initiative. The alterations are listed in the following table:

Revisions to the Text of the Proposed Amendments in Final Adoption

Section Revised	Source(s) of Revision(s)	Revision(s)
811.719(a)(2)(B)	JCAR	Added comma before "provided"

ILLINOIS REGISTER 2795

POLLUTION CONTROL BOARD

NOTICE OF ADOPTED AMENDMENTS

811.719(a)(3)	JCAR, Board	Added comma before last element of the series "and any other environmental obligation ..."; added comma before parenthetical "as described ."
811.719(b)(1)(A)(i)	JCAR	Changed comma to a semicolon to separate major elements of a series
811.719(b)(1)(B)	JCAR	Added definite article "the" before "owner or operator"
811.719(b)(2)	JCAR	Changed effective date to February 17, 1999, to reflect filing date; added a closing comma to complete offsetting the parenthetical "whichever is later"
811.719(b)(3)	JCAR	Corrected to possessive "owner's"
811.719(b)(4)(A)	Agency, Board	Added commas to offset parenthetical "as specified in this Subpart G"; corrected "this Section" to "this Subpart G"
811.719(b)(4)(B)	Agency	Corrected "this Section" to "this Subpart G"
811.719(b)(5)	Agency	Corrected "this Section" to "this Subpart G"
811.719(b)(6)	Agency	Corrected "this Section" to "this Subpart G"
811.719(c)	JCAR, Board	Deleted conjunction "or" from before "the sum of ...", since this is not the last element of the series; removed "part" from Code of Federal Register references (twice)
811.720(b)	JCAR	Changed effective date to February 17, 1999, to reflect filing date; added a closing comma to complete offsetting the parenthetical "whichever is later"; added comma after

ILLINOIS REGISTER 2796

POLLUTION CONTROL BOARD

NOTICE OF ADOPTED AMENDMENTS

		"Section 811.324" to offset parenthetical "in the case of ..."
811.720(c)(1)(A)	JCAR, Board	Removed two commas offsetting second element of a series "or pay a third party to perform" as a parenthetical
811.720(c)	JCAR	Changed "within 120 days of" to "within 120 days after"

12) Have all the changes agreed upon by the Board and JCAR been made as indicated in the agreements issued by JCAR? Section 22.40(a) of the Environmental Protection Act provides that Section 5 of the Administrative Procedure Act shall not apply. Because this rulemaking is not subject to Section 6 of the APA, it is not subject to first notice or to second notice review by JCAR.

13) Will these amendments replace emergency amendments currently in effect? No

14) Are there any other amendments pending on this Part? No

15) Summary and purpose of amendments: A more detailed description is contained in the Board's opinion and order of February 4, 1999, in R99-1, which opinion and order is available from the address below. Section 22.40 of the Environmental Protection Act provides that Section 5 of the Administrative Procedure Act shall not apply. Because this rulemaking is not subject to Section 5 of the APA, it is not subject to first notice or to second notice review by JCAR.

The R99-1 proceeding updates the Board's RCRA Subtitle D municipal solid waste landfill rules to correspond with a single set of amendments adopted by USEPA that appeared in the Federal Register during the period January 1, 1998, through June 30, 1998. That single action is summarized as follows:

63 Fed. Reg. 17706 (April 10, 1998)

USEPA adopted amendments that allow private owners and operators of MSWLF facilities to use two additional mechanisms for establishing financial assurance for facility closure, post-closure care, and corrective action. The added mechanisms are a corporate financial test for self-assurance and a corporate guarantee by a guarantor that has a "substantial business relationship" with the owner or operator.

The Board has incorporated the two added financial mechanisms now allowed by USEPA for privately-owned and operated MSWLF facilities.

16) Information and questions regarding these adopted amendments shall be

POLLUTION CONTROL BOARD

NOTICE OF ADOPTED AMENDMENTS

directed to:

Michael J. McCambridge
Attorney
Illinois Pollution Control Board
100 W. Randolph 11-500
Chicago IL 60601
312-814-6924

Request copies of the Board's opinion and order of February 4, 1999 from Victoria Agyeman at 312-814-3620.

The full text of the adopted amendments begins on the next page:

POLLUTION CONTROL BOARD

NOTICE OF ADOPTED AMENDMENTS

TITLE 35: ENVIRONMENTAL PROTECTION
SUBTITLE G: WASTE DISPOSAL
CHAPTER I: POLLUTION CONTROL BOARD
SUBCHAPTER i: SOLID WASTE AND SPECIAL WASTE HAULING

PART 811
STANDARDS FOR NEW SOLID WASTE LANDFILLS

SUBPART A: GENERAL STANDARDS FOR ALL LANDFILLS

Section
811.101 Scope and Applicability
811.102 Location Standards
811.103 Surface Water Drainage
811.104 Survey Controls
811.105 Compaction
811.106 Daily Cover
811.107 Operating Standards
811.108 Salvaging
811.109 Boundary Control
811.110 Closure and Written Closure Plan
811.111 Postclosure Maintenance

SUBPART B: INERT WASTE LANDFILLS

Section
811.201 Scope and Applicability
811.202 Determination of Contaminated Leachate
811.203 Design Period
811.204 Final Cover
811.205 Final Slope and Stabilization
811.206 Leachate Sampling
811.207 Load Checking

SUBPART C: PUTRESCIBLE AND CHEMICAL WASTE LANDFILLS

Section
811.301 Scope and Applicability
811.302 Facility Location
811.303 Design Period
811.304 Foundation and Mass Stability Analysis
811.305 Foundation Construction
811.306 Liner Systems
811.307 Leachate Drainage System
811.308 Leachate Collection System
811.309 Leachate Treatment and Disposal System
811.310 Landfill Gas Monitoring
811.311 Landfill Gas Management System

ILLINOIS REGISTER 2799

POLLUTION CONTROL BOARD

NOTICE OF ADOPTED AMENDMENTS

811.312   Landfill Gas Processing and Disposal System
811.313   Intermediate Cover
811.314   Final Cover System
811.315   Hydrogeological Site Investigations
811.316   Plugging and Sealing of Drill Holes
811.317   Groundwater Impact Assessment
811.318   Design, Construction, and Operation of Groundwater Monitoring Systems
811.319   Groundwater Monitoring Programs
811.320   Groundwater Quality Standards
811.321   Waste Placement
811.322   Final Slope and Stabilization
811.323   Load Checking Program
811.324   Corrective Action Measures for MSWLF Units
811.325   Selection of remedy for MSWLF Units
811.326   Implementation of the corrective action program at MSWLF Units

SUBPART D: MANAGEMENT OF SPECIAL WASTES AT LANDFILLS

Section
811.401   Scope and Applicability
811.402   Notice to Generators and Transporters
811.403   Special Waste Manifests
811.404   Identification Record
811.405   Recordkeeping Requirements
811.406   Procedures for Excluding Regulated Hazardous Wastes

SUBPART E: CONSTRUCTION QUALITY ASSURANCE PROGRAMS

Section
811.501   Scope and Applicability
811.502   Duties and Qualifications of Key Personnel
811.503   Inspection Activities
811.504   Sampling Requirements
811.505   Documentation
811.506   Foundations and Subbases
811.507   Compacted Earth Liners
811.508   Geomembranes
811.509   Leachate Collection Systems

SUBPART G: FINANCIAL ASSURANCE

Section
811.700   Scope, Applicability and Definitions
811.701   Upgrading Financial Assurance
811.702   Release of Financial Institution
811.703   Application of Proceeds and Appeals
811.704   Closure and Postclosure Care Cost Estimates
811.705   Revision of Cost Estimate

ILLINOIS REGISTER 2800

POLLUTION CONTROL BOARD

NOTICE OF ADOPTED AMENDMENTS

811.706   Mechanisms for Financial Assurance
811.707   Use of Multiple Financial Mechanisms
811.708   Use of a Financial Mechanism for Multiple Sites
811.709   Trust Fund for Unrelated Sites
811.710   Trust Fund
811.711   Surety Bond Guaranteeing Payment
811.712   Surety Bond Guaranteeing Performance
811.713   Letter of Credit
811.714   Closure Insurance
811.715   Self-Insurance for Non-commercial Sites
811.716   Local Government Financial Test
811.717   Local Government Guarantee
811.718   Discounting
811.719   Corporate Financial Test
811.720   Corporate Guarantee

APPENDIX A   Financial Assurance Forms

ILLUSTRATION A   Trust Agreement
ILLUSTRATION B   Certificate of Acknowledgment
ILLUSTRATION C   Forfeiture Bond
ILLUSTRATION D   Performance Bond
ILLUSTRATION E   Irrevocable Standby Letter of Credit
ILLUSTRATION F   Certificate of Insurance for Closure and/or Postclosure Care
ILLUSTRATION G   Operator's Bond Without Surety
ILLUSTRATION H   Operator's Bond With Parent Surety
ILLUSTRATION I   Letter from Chief Financial Officer

APPENDIX B   State-Federal MSWLF Regulations Correlation Table
              Section-by-Section---correlation--between--the--Standards-of-the
              RCRA-Subtitle-D-MSWLF-regulations-and-the-Board's--nonhazardous
              waste-landfill-regulations.

AUTHORITY: Implementing Sections 5, 21, 21.1, 22, 22.17 and 28.1 and
authorized by Section 27 of the Environmental Protection Act [415 ILCS 5/5, 21,
21.1, 22, 22.17, 28.1, and 27].

SOURCE: Adopted in R88-7 at 14 Ill. Reg. 15861, effective September 18, 1990;
amended in R92-19 at 17 Ill. Reg. 12413, effective July 19, 1993; amended in
R93-10 at 18 Ill. Reg. 1308, effective January 13, 1994; expedited correction
at 18 Ill. Reg. 7504, effective July 19, 1993; amended in R90-26 at 18 Ill.
Reg. 12481, effective August 1, 1994; amended in R95-13 at 19 Ill. Reg. 12257,
effective August 15, 1995; amended in R96-1 at 20 Ill. Reg. 12000, effective
August 15, 1996; amended in R97-20 at 21 Ill. Reg. 15831, effective November
25, 1997; amended in R98-9 at 22 Ill. Reg. 11491, effective June 23, 1998;
amended in R99-1 at 23 Ill. Reg. 2734 , effective
FEB 19 1999 .

ILLINOIS REGISTER 2801
99

POLLUTION CONTROL BOARD

NOTICE OF ADOPTED AMENDMENTS

NOTE: In this Part, superscript numbers or letters are denoted by parentheses; subscript are denoted by brackets.

SUBPART G: FINANCIAL ASSURANCE

Section 811.706 Mechanisms for Financial Assurance

a) The owner or operator of a waste disposal site may utilize any of the mechanisms listed in subsections (a)(1) through (a)(10) (a)(6) to provide financial assurance for closure and postclosure care, and for corrective action at an MSWLF unit. An owner or operator of an MSWLF unit shall also meet the requirements of subsections (b), (c), and (d). The mechanisms are as follows:
   1) A trust <u>fund</u> Fund (see Section 811.710);
   2) A surety <u>bond guaranteeing payment</u> Bond-Guaranteeing-Payment (see Section 811.711);
   3) A surety <u>bond guaranteeing performance</u> Bond---Guaranteeing Performance (see Section 811.712);
   4) A letter of <u>credit</u> Credit (see Section 811.713);
   5) Closure <u>insurance</u> Insurance (see Section 811.714);
   6) Self-insurance (see Section 811.715);
   7) Local <u>government financial test</u> Government-Financial-Test (see Section 811.716); or
   8) Local <u>government guarantee</u> Government--Guarantee (see Section 811.717)<u>;</u>.
   <u>9) Corporate financial test (see Section 811.719); or</u>
   <u>10) Corporate guarantee (see Section 811.720).</u>
b) The owner or operator of an MSWLF unit shall ensure that the language of the mechanisms listed in subsection (a), when used for providing financial assurance for closure, postclosure, and corrective action, satisfies the following:
   1) The amount of funds assured is sufficient to cover the costs of closure, post-closure care, and corrective action; and
   2) The funds will be available in a timely fashion when needed.
c) The owner or operator of an MSWLF unit shall provide financial assurance utilizing one or more of the mechanisms listed in subsection (a) within the following dates:
   1) By April 9, 1997, or such later date granted pursuant to Section 811.700(g), or prior to the initial receipt of solid waste, whichever is later, in the case of closure and post-closure care; or
   2) No later than 120 days after the remedy has been selected in accordance with the requirements of Section 811.325, in the case of corrective action.
d) The owner or operator shall provide continuous coverage until the owner or operator is released from the financial assurance requirements pursuant to 35 Ill. Adm. Code 813.403(b) or Section 811.326.

ILLINOIS REGISTER 2802
99

POLLUTION CONTROL BOARD

NOTICE OF ADOPTED AMENDMENTS

BOARD NOTE: Subsections (b) and (c) are derived from 40 CFR 258.74(1) (1996). Amendments prompted by amendments to 40 CFR 258.74(a)(5) (1996). P.A. 89-200, signed by the Governor on July 21, 1995 and effective January 1, 1996, amended the deadline for financial assurance for MSWLFs from April 9, 1995 to the date that the federal financial assurance requirements actually become effective, which was April 9, 1997. On November 27, 1996 (61 Fed. Reg. 60327), USEPA added 40 CFR 258.70(c) (1996), codified here as Section 811.700(g), to allow states to waive the compliance deadline until April 9, 1998.

(Source: <u>Amended</u> at 23 Ill. Reg. 2794 , effective FEB 17 1999)

Section 811.707 Use of Multiple Financial Mechanisms

An owner or operator may satisfy the requirements of this Subpart by establishing more than one financial mechanism per site. These mechanisms are limited to trust funds, surety bonds guaranteeing payment, letters of credit and insurance. The mechanisms must be as specified in 35 Ill. Adm. Code 811.710, 811.711 <u>and</u> 811.713 <u>through 811.720</u> ,-811.714,-811.715,-811.716,--and 811.717, as applicable, except that it is the combination of mechanisms, rather than the single mechanism, that must provide financial assurance for an aggregate amount at least equal to the current cost estimate for closure, post-closure care or corrective action, except that mechanisms guaranteeing performance, rather than payment, may not be combined with other instruments. The owner or operator may use any or all of the mechanisms to provide for closure and postclosure care of the site or corrective action.

(Source: <u>Amended</u>, at 23 Ill. Reg. 2794 , effective FEB 17 1999)

<u>Section 811.719 Corporate Financial Test</u>

<u>An MSWLF owner or operator that satisfies the requirements of this Section may demonstrate financial assurance up to the amount specified in this Section as follows:</u>
   <u>a) Financial component.</u>
      <u>1) The owner or operator must satisfy one of the following three conditions:</u>
         <u>A) A current rating for its senior unsubordinated debt of AAA, AA, A, or BBB as issued by Standard and Poor's or Aaa, Aa, A or Baa as issued by Moody's; or</u>
         <u>B) A ratio of less than 1.5 comparing total liabilities to net worth; or</u>
         <u>C) A ratio of greater than 0.10 comparing the sum of net income plus depreciation, depletion and amortization, minus $10 million, to total liabilities.</u>
      <u>2) The tangible net worth of the owner or operator must be greater</u>

POLLUTION CONTROL BOARD

NOTICE OF ADOPTED AMENDMENTS

than:

> A) The sum of the current closure, post-closure care, and
> corrective action cost estimates and any other environmental
> obligations, including guarantees, covered by a financial
> test plus $10 million except as provided in subsection
> (a)(2)(B) of this Section.
>
> B) $10 million in net worth plus the amount of any guarantees
> that have not been recognized as liabilities on the
> financial statements, provided all of the current closure,
> post-closure care, and corrective action costs and any other
> environmental obligations covered by a financial test are
> recognized as liabilities on the owner's or operator's
> audited financial statements, and subject to the approval of
> the Agency.
>
> 3) The owner or operator must have assets located in the United
> States amounting to at least the sum of current closure,
> post-closure care, and corrective action cost estimates and any
> other environmental obligations covered by a financial test as
> described in subsection (c) of this Section.
>
> b) Recordkeeping and reporting requirements.
>
> 1) The owner or operator must place the following items into the
> facility's operating record:
>
>> A) A letter signed by the owner's or operator's chief financial
>> officer that includes the following:
>>
>>> i) All the current cost estimates covered by a financial
>>> test, including, but not limited to, cost estimates
>>> required for municipal solid waste management
>>> facilities under this Part; cost estimates required
>>> for UIC facilities under 35 Ill. Adm. Code 730, if
>>> applicable; cost estimates required for petroleum
>>> underground storage tank facilities under 40 CFR 280,
>>> if applicable; cost estimates required for PCB storage
>>> facilities under 40 CFR 761, if applicable; and cost
>>> estimates required for hazardous waste treatment,
>>> storage, and disposal facilities under 35 Ill. Adm.
>>> Code 724 or 725, if applicable; and
>>>
>>> ii) Evidence demonstrating that the firm meets the
>>> conditions of subsection (a)(1)(A), (a)(1)(B), or
>>> (a)(1)(C) of this Section and subsection (a)(2) and
>>> (a)(3) of this Section.
>>
>> B) A copy of the independent certified public accountant's
>> unqualified opinion of the owner's or operator's financial
>> statements for the latest completed fiscal year. To be
>> eligible to use the financial test, the owner's or
>> operator's financial statements must receive an unqualified
>> opinion from the independent certified public accountant.
>> An adverse opinion, disclaimer of opinion, or other
>> qualified opinion will be cause for disallowance, with the

potential exception for qualified opinions provided in the
next sentence. The Agency shall evaluate qualified opinions
on a case-by-case basis and allow use of the financial test
in cases where the Agency deems that the matters that form
the basis for the qualification are insufficient to warrant
disallowance of the test. If the Agency does not allow use
of the test, the owner or operator shall provide alternative
financial assurance that meets the requirements of this
Section.

> C) If the chief financial officer's letter providing evidence
> of financial assurance includes financial data showing that
> the owner or operator satisfies subsection (a)(1)(B) or
> (a)(1)(C) of this Section that are different from data in
> the audited financial statements referred to in subsection
> (b)(1)(B) of this Section or any other audited financial
> statement or data filed with the federal Security Exchange
> Commission, then a special report from the owner's or
> operator's independent certified public accountant to the
> owner or operator is required. The special report must be
> based upon an agreed upon procedures engagement in
> accordance with professional auditing standards and shall
> describe the procedures performed in comparing the data in
> the chief financial officer's letter derived from the
> independently audited, year-end financial statements for the
> latest fiscal year with the amounts in such financial
> statements, the findings of that comparison, and the reasons
> for any differences.
>
> D) If the chief financial officer's letter provides a
> demonstration that the firm has assured for environmental
> obligations, as provided in subsection (a)(2)(B) of this
> Section, then the letter shall include a report from the
> independent certified public accountant that verifies that
> all of the environmental obligations covered by a financial
> test have been recognized as liabilities on the audited
> financial statements, how these obligations have been
> measured and reported, and that the tangible net worth of
> the firm is at least $10 million plus the amount of any
> guarantees provided.
>
> 2) An owner or operator shall place the items specified in
> subsection (b)(1) of this Section in the operating record and
> notify the Agency in writing that these items have been placed in
> the operating record before the initial receipt of waste or
> before February 17, 1999, whichever is later, in the case of
> closure and post-closure care, or no later than 120 days after
> the corrective action remedy has been selected, in accordance
> with the requirements of Section 811.324.
> BOARD NOTE: Corresponding 40 CFR 258.74(e)(2)(11) provides that
> this requirement is effective "before the initial receipt of

POLLUTION CONTROL BOARD

NOTICE OF ADOPTED AMENDMENTS

waste or before the effective date of the requirements of this Section (April 9, 1997 or October 9, 1997 for MSWLF units meeting the conditions of Sec. 258.1(f)(1)), whichever is later." The Board has instead inserted the date on which these amendments are to be filed and become effective in Illinois.

3) After the initial placement of items specified in subsection (b)(1) of this Section in the operating record, the owner or operator must annually update the information and place updated information in the operating record within 90 days following the close of the owner's or operator's fiscal year. The Agency shall provide up to an additional 45 days for an owner or operator who can demonstrate that 90 days is insufficient time to acquire audited financial statements. The updated information must consist of all items specified in subsection (b)(1) of this Section.

4) The owner or operator is no longer required to submit the items specified in this subsection (b) or comply with the requirements of this section when either of the following occurs:

   A) It substitutes alternative financial assurance, as specified in this Section that is not subject to these recordkeeping and reporting requirements; or

   B) It is released from the requirements of this Section in accordance with Sections 811.700 and 811.706.

5) If the owner or operator no longer meets the requirements of subsection (a) of this Section, the owner or operator shall obtain alternative financial assurance that meets the requirements of this Section within 120 days following the close of the facility's fiscal year. The owner or operator shall also place the required submissions for the alternative financial assurance in the facility operating record and notify the Agency that it no longer meets the criteria of the financial test and that it has obtained alternative financial assurance.

6) The Agency may require the owner or operator to provide reports of its financial condition in addition to or including current financial test documentation specified in subsection (b) of this Section at any time it has a reasonable belief that the owner or operator may no longer meet the requirements of subsection (a) of this Section. If the Agency finds that the owner or operator no longer meets the requirements of subsection (a) of this Section, the owner or operator shall provide alternative financial assurance that meets the requirements of this Section.

c) Calculation of costs to be assured. When calculating the current cost estimates for closure, post-closure care, or corrective action, or the sum of the combination of such costs to be covered, and any other environmental obligations assured by a financial test referred to in this Section, the owner or operator shall include cost estimates required for municipal solid waste management facilities under this Part, as well as cost estimates required for the following

environmental obligations, if it assures them through a financial test: obligations associated with UIC facilities under 35 Ill. Adm. Code 730; petroleum underground storage tank facilities under 40 CFR 280; PCB storage facilities under 40 CFR 761; and hazardous waste treatment, storage, and disposal facilities under 35 Ill. Adm. Code 724 or 725.

(Source: Added at 23 Ill. Reg. 2/94 5, effective FEB 17 '99)

Section 811.720 Corporate Guarantee

a) An owner or operator of an MSWLF may meet the requirements of 35 Ill. Adm. Code 811.700 and 811.706 by obtaining a written guarantee. The guarantor must be the direct or higher-tier parent corporation of the owner or operator, or a firm whose parent corporation is also the parent corporation of the owner or operator, or a firm with a "substantial business relationship" with the owner or operator. The guarantor must meet the requirements for owners or operators in Section 811.719 and must comply with the terms of the guarantee. The owner or operator shall place a certified copy of the guarantee in the facility's operating record along with a copy of the letter from the guarantor's chief financial officer and copies of the accountants' opinions. If the guarantor's parent corporation is also the parent corporation of the owner or operator, the letter from the guarantor's chief financial officer must describe the value received in consideration of the guarantee. If the guarantor is a firm with a "substantial business relationship" with the owner or operator, this letter must describe this "substantial business relationship" and the value received in consideration of the guarantee.

b) The guarantee must be effective and all required submissions placed in the operating record before the initial receipt of waste or before February 17, 1999, whichever is later, in the case of closure and post-closure care, or no later than 120 days after the corrective action remedy has been selected in accordance with the requirements of Section 811.324, in the case of corrective action.
BOARD NOTE: Corresponding 40 CFR 258.74(g)(2) provides that this requirement is effective "before the initial receipt of waste or before the effective date of the requirements of this Section (April 9, 1997 or October 9, 1997 for MSWLF units meeting the conditions of Sec. 258.1(f)(1)), whichever is later." The Board has instead inserted the date on which these amendments are to be filed and become effective in Illinois.

c) The terms of the guarantee must provide as follows:

   1) If the owner or operator fails to perform closure, post-closure care, or corrective action of a facility covered by the guarantee, the guarantor will:

      A) Perform, or pay a third party to perform closure,

ILLINOIS REGISTER 2807

POLLUTION CONTROL BOARD

NOTICE OF ADOPTED AMENDMENTS

post-closure care, and corrective action, as required (performance guarantee); or

B) Establish a fully funded trust fund, as specified in Section 811.709 or 811.710, in the name of the owner or operator (payment guarantee).

2) The guarantee will remain in force for as long as the owner or operator must comply with the applicable financial assurance requirements of this Subpart unless the guarantor sends prior notice of cancellation by certified mail to the owner or operator and to the Agency. Cancellation may not occur, however, during the 120 days beginning on the date on which the owner or operator and the Agency have both received the notice of cancellation, as evidenced by the return receipts.

3) If the guarantor gives notice of cancellation, the owner or operator shall obtain alternative financial assurance, place evidence of that alternative financial assurance in the facility operating record, and notify the Agency within 90 days following receipt of the cancellation notice by the owner or operator and the Agency. If the owner or operator fails to obtain alternative financial assurance within the 90-day period, the guarantor must provide that alternative assurance within 120 days after the cancellation notice, obtain alternative financial assurance, place evidence of the alternative assurance in the facility operating record, and notify the Agency.

d) If a corporate guarantor no longer meets the requirements of Section 811.710(a), the owner or operator shall obtain alternative assurance, place evidence of the alternative assurance in the facility operating record, and notify the Agency within 90 days. If the owner or operator fails to provide alternative financial assurance within the 90-day period, the guarantor shall provide that alternative assurance within the next 30 days.

e) The owner or operator is no longer required to meet the requirements of this Section when:

1) The owner or operator substitutes alternative financial assurance, as specified in this Subpart G; or

2) The owner or operator is released from the requirements of this Subpart G in accordance with Sections 811.700 and 811.706.

(Source: Added at ___ 23 Ill. Reg. 2794 , effective ___)

ILLINOIS REGISTER 2808

POLLUTION CONTROL BOARD

NOTICE OF ADOPTED AMENDMENTS

Section 811.APPENDIX B State-Federal MSWLF Regulations Correlation Table
Section-by-Section-correlation-between-the-Standards-of--the--RCRA--Subtitle--D MSWLF-regulations-and-the-Board's-nonhazardous-waste-landfill-regulations.

RCRA SUBTITLE D REGULATIONS	ILLINOIS LANDFILL REGULATIONS
I. SUBPART A: General	
1) Purpose, Scope, and Applicability (40 CFR 258.1)	1) NL(1): Sections 811.101 811.301, 811.401, 811.501, and 811.700. EL(2): Section 814.101.
2) Definitions (40 CFR 258.2)	2) Section 810.103.
II. SUBPART B: Location Restrictions	
1) Airport safety (40 CFR 258.10)	1) NL(1): Section 811.302(e). EL(2): Section 814.302(c) and 814.402(c).
2) Floodplains. (40 CFR 258.11)	2) NL(1): Section 811.102(b). EL(2): Section 814.302 and 814.402.
3) Wetlands. (40 CFR 258.12)	3) NL(1): Sections 811.102(d), 811.102(e), and 811.103. EL(2): Section 814.302 and 814.402.
4) Fault areas. (40 CFR 258.13)	4) NL(1): Section 811.304 and 811.305. EL(2): Section 814.302 and 814.402.
5) Seismic impact zones. (40 CFR 258.14)	5) See above.
6) Unstable areas. (40 CFR 258.15)	6) NL(1): Sections 811.304 and 811.305. EL(2): Sections 811.302(c) and 811.402(c).
7) Closure of existing MSWL units. (40 CFR 258.16)	7) EL(2): Sections 814.301 and 814.401.
III. SUBPART C: Operating Criteria	

POLLUTION CONTROL BOARD

NOTICE OF ADOPTED AMENDMENTS

1) Procedures for excluding the receipt of hazardous waste. (40 CFR 258.20)
  1) NL(1): Section 811.323. EL(2): Sections 814.302 and 814.402.

2) Cover material requirements. (40 CFR 258.21)
  2) NL(1): Section 811.106. EL(2): Sections 814.302 and 814.402.

3) Disease vector control. (40 CFR 258.22)
  3) NL(1): Section 811.107(i). EL(2): Sections 814.302 and 814.402.

4) Explosive gas control. (40 CFR 258.23)
  4) NL(1): Sections 811.310, 811.311, and 811.312. EL(2): Sections 814.302 and 814.402.

5) Air criteria. (40 CFR 258.24)
  5) NL(1): Section 811.107(b), 811.310, and 811.311. EL(2): Sections 814.302 and 814.402.

6) Access requirements. (40 CFR 258.25)
  6) NL(1): Section 811.109. EL(2): Sections 814.302 and 814.402.

7) Run-on/run-off control system. (40 CFR 258.26)
  7) NL(1): Section 811.103. EL(2): Sections 814.302 and 814.402.

8) Surface water requirements. (40 CFR 258.27)
  8) Same as above.

9) Liquids restrictions. (40 CFR 258.28)
  9) NL(1): Section 811.107(m). EL(2): Sections 814.302 and 814.402.

10) Recordkeeping requirements. (40 CFR 258.29)
  10) NL(1): Sections 811.112, and Parts 812 and 813. EL(2): Sections 814.302 and 814.402.

IV. SUBPART D: Design criteria (40 CFR 258.40)
  IV) NL(1): 811.303, 811.304, 811.305, 811.306, 811.307, 811.308, 811.309, 811.315, 811.316, 811.317, and 811.Subpart E. EL(2): Sections 814.302 and 814.402.

V. SUBPART E: Groundwater Monitoring and Corrective Action

POLLUTION CONTROL BOARD

NOTICE OF ADOPTED AMENDMENTS

1) Applicability.
  1) NL(1): 35 Section 811.319 (a)(1). EL(2): Sections 814.302 and 814.402.

2) Groundwater monitoring systems. (40 CFR 258.51)
  2) NL(1): Sections 811.318 and 811.320(d). EL(2): Sections 814.302 and 814.402.

3) Groundwater sampling and analysis. (40 CFR 258.53)
  3) NL(1): Section 811.318(e), 811.320(d), 811.320(e). EL(2): Sections 814.302 and 814.402.

4) Detection monitoring program. (40 CFR 258.54)
  4) NL(1): Section 811.319(a). EL(2): Sections 814.302 and 814.402.

5) Assessment monitoring program. (40 CFR 258.55)
  5) NL(1): Section 811.319(b). EL(2): Sections 814.302 and 814.402.

6) Assessment of corrective measures. (40 CFR 258.56)
  6) NL(1): Sections 811.319(d) and 811.324. EL(2): Sections 814.302 and 814.402.

7) Selection of remedy. (40 CFR 258.57)
  7) NL(1): Sections 811.319(d) and 811.325. EL(2): Sections 814.302 and 814.402.

8) Implementation of the corrective action program. (40 CFR 258.58)
  8) NL(1): Sections 811.319(d) and 811.325. EL(2): Sections 814.302 and 814.403.

VI. SUBPART F: Closure and Post-Closure Care

1) Closure criteria. (40 CFR 258.60)
  1) NL(1): Sections 811.110, 811.315 and 811.323. EL(2): Sections 814.302 and 814.402.

2) Post-closure care requirements. (40 CFR 258.61)
  2) NL(1): Section 811.111. EL(2): Sections 814.302 and 814.402.

VII. SUBPART G: Financial Assurance Criteria

1) Applicability and effective date. (40 CFR 258.70)
  1) NL(1): Section 811.700. EL(2): Sections 814.302 and 814.402.

ILLINOIS REGISTER 2811
99

POLLUTION CONTROL BOARD

NOTICE OF ADOPTED AMENDMENTS

2) Financial assurance for   2) NL(1): Sections 811.701 through
   closure. (40 CFR 258.71)   811.705. EL(2): Sections 814.302
                                       and 814.402.

3) Financial assurance for   3) Same as (2).
   post-closure. (40 CFR 258.72)

4) Financial assurance for   4) Same as (2).
   corrective action. (40 CFR
   258.73)

5) Allowable mechanisms. (40   5) NL(1): Section 811.706
   CFR 258.74 and 258.75)   through 811.720919. EL(2):
                                      Sections 814.302 and
                                      814.402.

1 - NL: New Landfill; 2 - EL: Existing Landfill and Lateral Expansions.

    (Source: Amended   at   23   Ill.   Reg. 2794 =, effective

---

ILLINOIS REGISTER 2812
99

DEPARTMENT OF CENTRAL MANAGEMENT SERVICES

NOTICE OF EMERGENCY AMENDMENTS

1) Heading of the Part: Standard Procurement

2) Code Citation: 44 Ill Adm. Code 1

3) Section Number: Emergency Action:
    1.2020   Amend

4) Statutory Authority: 30 ILCS 500

5) Effective Date of Amendments: February 16, 1999

6) If this emergency rule is to expire before end of the 150-day period,
    please specify the date on which it is to expire: Not applicable

7) Date Filed with the Index Department: February 16, 1999

8) A copy of the emergency amendments, including any material incorporated by
    reference, is on file in the agency's principal office and is available
    for public inspection.

9) Reason for Emergency: To ensure that concessions at the Illinois State
    Fairgrounds in Springfield and DuQuoin will be available.

10) A Complete Description of the Subjects and Issues Involved: Raises the
    small purchase threshold from $10,000 to $25,000 per year solely for
    concession contracts at the Illinois State Fairgrounds in Springfield and
    DuQuoin when such concessions offer or display exhibits, goods, or
    services to the general public. The threshold will be raised through the
    normal rulemaking process for all other purposes.

11) Are there any proposed amendments to this Part pending: No

12) Statement of Statewide Policy Objectives: Rulemaking does not affect units
    of local government.

13) Information and questions regarding this amendment shall be directed to:

        Stephen W. Seiple
        720 Stratton Office Building
        Springfield IL 62706
        217/782-9669

The full text of the emergency amendments begins on the next page:

DEPARTMENT OF CENTRAL MANAGEMENT SERVICES

NOTICE OF EMERGENCY AMENDMENTS

SUBTITLE A: PROCUREMENT AND CONTRACT PROVISIONS
CHAPTER I: DEPARTMENT OF CENTRAL MANAGEMENT SERVICES

PART 1
STANDARD PROCUREMENT

SUBPART A: GENERAL

Section
1.01 Title
1.05 Policy
1.08 Purpose and Implementation of This Part
1.10 Application
1.15 Definition of Terms Used in This Part
1.25 Property Rights
1.30 Constitutional Officers, and Legislative and Judicial Branches

SUBPART B: PROCUREMENT RULES

Section
1.525 Rules

SUBPART C: PROCUREMENT AUTHORITY

Section
1.1005 Exercise of Procurement Authority
1.1010 Appointment of State Purchasing Officer
1.1030 Associate Procurement Officers
1.1040 Central Procurement Authority of the CPO
1.1050 Procurement Authority of the SPO; Limitations
1.1060 Delegation
1.1070 Toll Highway Authority
1.1075 Department of Natural Resources
1.1080 Illinois Mathematics and Science Academy

SUBPART D: PUBLICIZING PROCUREMENT ACTIONS

Section
1.1510 Illinois Procurement Bulletin
1.1525 Bulletin Content
1.1550 Official State Newspaper
1.1560 Supplemental Notice
1.1570 Error in Notice
1.1580 Direct Solicitation
1.1590 Retention of Bulletin Information

SUBPART E: SOURCE SELECTION AND CONTRACT FORMATION

DEPARTMENT OF CENTRAL MANAGEMENT SERVICES

NOTICE OF EMERGENCY AMENDMENTS

Section
1.2005 General Provisions
1.2010 Competitive Sealed Bidding
1.2012 Multi-Step Sealed Bidding
1.2015 Competitive Sealed Proposals
1.2020 Small Purchases
EMERGENCY
1.2025 Sole Economically Feasible Source Procurement
1.2030 Emergency Procurements
1.2035 Competitive Selection Procedures for Professional and Artistic Services
1.2036 Other Methods of Source Selection
1.2037 Tie Bids and Proposals
1.2038 Mistakes
1.2040 Cancellation of Solicitations; Rejection of Bids or Proposals

SUBPART F: SUPPLIERS, PREQUALIFICATION AND RESPONSIBILITY

Section
1.2043 Suppliers
1.2044 Vendor List/Required Use
1.2045 Prequalification
1.2046 Responsibility

SUBPART G: BID, PROPOSAL AND PERFORMANCE SECURITY

Section
1.2047 Security Requirements

SUBPART H: SPECIFICATIONS AND SAMPLES

Section
1.2050 Specifications and Samples

SUBPART I: CONTRACT TYPE

Section
1.2055 Types of Contracts

SUBPART J: DURATION OF CONTRACTS

Section
1.2060 Duration of Contracts - General

SUBPART K: CONTRACT MATTERS

Section
1.2560 Prevailing Wage

ILLINOIS REGISTER

DEPARTMENT OF CENTRAL MANAGEMENT SERVICES

NOTICE OF EMERGENCY AMENDMENTS

1.2570   Equal Employment Opportunity; Affirmative Action

SUBPART L: CONTRACT PRICING

Section
1.2800   All Costs Included

SUBPART M: CONSTRUCTION AND CONSTRUCTION RELATED PROFESSIONAL
SERVICES

Section
1.3005   Construction and Construction Related Professional Services

SUBPART N: REAL PROPERTY LEASES AND CAPITAL IMPROVEMENT LEASES

Section
1.4005   Real Property Leases and Capital Improvement Leases

SUBPART O: PREFERENCES

Section
1.4505   Procurement Preferences
1.4510   Resident Bidder Preference
1.4530   Correctional Industries
1.4535   Sheltered Workshops for the Disabled
1.4540   Gas Mileage
1.4545   Small Business
1.4570   Contracting with Businesses owned and Controlled by Minorities,
Females and Persons with Disabilities

SUBPART P: ETHICS

Section
1.5013   Conflicts of Interest
1.5015   Negotiations for Future Employment
1.5020   Exemptions
1.5030   Revolving Door
1.5035   Disclosure of Financial Interests and Potential Conflicts of Interest

SUBPART Q: CONCESSIONS

Section
1.5310   Concessions

SUBPART R: COMPLAINTS, PROTESTS AND REMEDIES

Section
1.5510   Complaints Against Vendors

DEPARTMENT OF CENTRAL MANAGEMENT SERVICES

NOTICE OF EMERGENCY AMENDMENTS

1.5520   Suspension
1.5530   Resolution of Contract Controversies
1.5540   Violation of Law or Rule
1.5550   Protests

SUBPART S: SUPPLY MANAGEMENT AND DISPOSITIONS

Section
1.6010   Supply Management and Dispositions

SUBPART T: GOVERNMENTAL JOINT PURCHASING

Section
1.6500   General
1.6510   No Agency Relationship
1.6520   Obligations of Participating Governmental Units
1.6530   Centralized Contracts - Estimated Quantities
1.6535   Centralized Contracts - Definite Quantities

SUBPART U: MISCELLANEOUS PROVISIONS OF GENERAL APPLICABILITY

Section
1.7000   Severability
1.7010   Government Furnished Property
1.7015   Inspections
1.7020   Records and Audits
1.7025   Written Determinations
1.7030   No Waiver of Sovereign Immunity

AUTHORITY: The Illinois Procurement Code [30 ILCS 500] (see P.A. 90-572).

SOURCE: Adopted at 7 Ill. Reg. 100, effective December 17, 1982; amended at 7
Ill. Reg. 13481, effective October 4, 1983; amended at 7 Ill. Reg. 13844,
effective October 12, 1983; codified at 8 Ill. Reg. 14941; Sections 1.2210,
1.2220, 1.2230, 1.2240 recodified to Section 1.2210 at 9 Ill. Reg. 6118;
amended at 10 Ill. Reg. 923, effective January 2, 1986; amended at 10 Ill. Reg.
18707, effective October 22, 1986; amended at 11 Ill. Reg. 7225, effective
April 6, 1987; amended at 11 Ill. Reg. 7595, effective April 14, 1987; amended
at 13 Ill. Reg. 17804, effective November 7, 1989; emergency amendment at 16
Ill. Reg. 13118, effective August 7, 1992, for a maximum of 150 days; amended
at 17 Ill. Reg. 600, effective January 5, 1993; amended at 17 Ill. Reg. 14576,
effective August 27, 1993; amended at 20 Ill. Reg. 9015, effective July 1,
1996; old Part repealed by emergency rulemaking at 22 Ill. Reg. 12632,
effective July 1, 1998, for a maximum of 150 days and new Part adopted by
emergency rulemaking at 22 Ill. Reg. 12726, effective July 1, 1998, for a
maximum of 150 days; old Part repealed and new Part adopted at 22 Ill. Reg.
20875, effective November 25, 1998; emergency amendment at 23 Ill. Reg.
2812, effective February 16, 1999, for a maximum of 150 days.

DEPARTMENT OF CENTRAL MANAGEMENT SERVICES

NOTICE OF EMERGENCY AMENDMENTS

SUBPART E: SOURCE SELECTION AND CONTRACT FORMATION

Section 1.2020 Small Purchases
EMERGENCY

a) Application
   1) Procurements of $10,000 or less for supplies or services, other than professional and artistic, and $30,000 or less for construction may be made using the method of source selection determined by the Procurement Officer to be most appropriate to the circumstances. For purposes of contracting for concessions at the Illinois State Fairgrounds in Springfield and DuQuoin of less than 15 days (excluding set up and dismantling) per location or event per year when such concessions offer or display exhibits, goods, or services to the general public, the small purchase threshold is $25,000.
   2) Procurements of less than $20,000 for professional and artistic services and that have a non-renewable term of one year or less may be made using the method of source selection determined by the Procurement Officer to be most appropriate to the circumstances.
   3) The CPO shall announce any change identified by the United States Department of Labor in the Consumer Price Index for All Urban Consumers for the period ending December 31, 1998, and for each year thereafter. That percentage change shall be used to calculate the small purchase maximums that shall be applicable for the fiscal year beginning July 1, 1999. The small purchase maximums shall be likewise recalculated for each July 1 thereafter.

b) In determining whether a contract is under the limit, the value of the contract for the full term and all optional renewals, determined in good faith, shall be utilized. The stated value of the supplies or services, plus any optional supplies and services, shall be utilized. Where the term is calculated month-to-month or in a similar fashion, the amount shall be calculated for a twelve month period.

c) If only a unit price or hourly rate is known, the contract shall be considered small and shall have a not to exceed limit applicable to the type of procurement (see subsection (a) above).

d) If, after signing the contract, the actual cost of completing the contract is determined to exceed the small purchase amount, and the Procurement Officer determines that a supplemental procurement is not economically feasible or practicable because of the immediacy of the agency's needs or other circumstances, the Procurement Officer must follow the procedures for sole source or emergency procurement, whichever is applicable, to complete the contract.

e) Procurement requirements shall not be artificially divided to avoid using the other source selection methods set forth in Section 20-5 of the Illinois Procurement Code.

f) If there is a repetitive need for small procurements of the same type, the Procurement Officer shall consider issuing a competitive sealed bid or proposal for procurement of those needs.

g) Agencies shall establish policies to control the use of this small purchase provision and shall make those policies available to the CPO upon request.

(Source: Amended by emergency rulemaking at 23 Ill. Reg. 2812, effective February 16, 1999, for a maximum of 150 days)

ILLINOIS REGISTER 2819
99

DEPARTMENT OF NATURAL RESOURCES

NOTICE OF PUBLIC HEARING ON PROPOSED AMENDMENTS

1) Heading of the Part: White-Tailed Deer Hunting by Use of Bow and Arrow

2) Code Citation: 17 Ill. Adm. Code 670

3) Register Citation to Notice of Proposed Amendments: 23 Ill. Reg. 833; January 22, 1999

4) Date, Time and Location of Public Hearing:

March 10, 1999
1:30 p.m.
Eagle Creek State Park Lodge
Findlay, Illinois

5) Other Pertinent Information:

Individuals who are unable to attend the public hearing but wish to comment on the Proposed Amendments should submit written comments by March 10, 1999, to:

Jack Price
Department of Natural Resources
524 S. Second Street
Springfield, IL 62701-1787
Telephone: 217/782-1809
Fax: 217/524-9640

All comments received will be fully considered by the agency.

ILLINOIS REGISTER 2820
99

JOINT COMMITTEE ON ADMINISTRATIVE RULES
ILLINOIS GENERAL ASSEMBLY

FILING PROHIBITION

STATE BOARD OF ELECTIONS

Heading of the Part: Established Political Party and Independent Candidate Nominating Petitions

Code Citation: 26 Ill Adm Code 201

Section Numbers: 201.60

Date Originally Published in the Illinois Register: 5/8/98
22 Ill Reg 7858

At its meeting on February 17, 1999, the Joint Committee on Administrative Rules voted to object to the above proposed rulemaking and prohibit its filing with the Secretary of State. The Committee found that the adoption of these rules would constitute a serious threat to the public interest, safety or welfare. The reason for the prohibition is as follows:

The Joint Committee objects to and prohibits the filing of the State Board of Elections' rulemaking entitled Established Political Party and Independent Candidate Nominating Petitions (26 Ill Adm Code 201; 22 Ill Reg 7858) because the Board is establishing by rule, without clear statutory authority, a process for review of nominating petitions, when the Election Code clearly prescribes another process for that purpose.

The proposed rules may not be filed with the Secretary of State or enforced by the State Board of Elections for any reason for 180 days following receipt of this certification and statement by the Secretary of State.

JOINT COMMITTEE ON ADMINISTRATIVE RULES
ILLINOIS GENERAL ASSEMBLY

FILING PROHIBITION

STATE BOARD OF ELECTIONS

Heading of the Part: New Political Party Nominating Petitions

Code Citation: 26 Ill Adm Code 202

Section Numbers: 202.60

Date Originally Published in the Illinois Register: 5/8/98
22 Ill Reg 7862

At its meeting on February 17, 1999, the Joint Committee on Administrative Rules voted to object to the above proposed rulemaking and prohibit its filing with the Secretary of State. The Committee found that the adoption of these rules would constitute a serious threat to the public interest, safety or welfare. The reason for the prohibition is as follows:

The Joint Committee objects to and prohibits the filing of the State Board of Elections' rulemaking entitled New Political Party Nominating Petitions (26 Ill Adm Code 202; 22 Ill Reg 7862) because the Board is establishing by rule, without clear statutory authority, a process for review of nominating petitions, when the Election Code clearly prescribes another process for that purpose.

The proposed rules may not be filed with the Secretary of State or enforced by the State Board of Elections for any reason for 180 days following receipt of this certification and statement by the Secretary of State.

JOINT COMMITTEE ON ADMINISTRATIVE RULES
ILLINOIS GENERAL ASSEMBLY

STATEMENT OF OBJECTION
TO PROPOSED RULEMAKING

DEPARTMENT OF PUBLIC HEALTH

Heading of the Part: Asbestos Abatement for Public and Private Schools and Commercial and Public Buildings

Code Citation: 77 Ill Adm Code 855

Section Numbers:

855.5	855.230	855.400	855.480	Appendix B
855.10	855.240	855.410	855.490	Illustration A
855.20	855.300	855.420	855.500	Illustration B
855.25	855.310	855.425	855.510	Illustration C
855.100	855.325	855.430	855.520	Illustration D
855.110	855.330	855.440	855.600	Illustration E
855.120	855.350	855.450	855.610	Illustration F
855.140	855.360	855.460	855.620	Illustration G
855.160	855.370	855.465	855.630	Illustration H
855.170	855.380	855.470	855.640	Illustration I
855.220	855.390	855.475	Appendix A	
			Illustration A	

Date Originally Published in the Illinois Register: 3/13/98
22 Ill Reg 4632

At its meeting on February 17, 1999, the Joint Committee on Administrative Rules objected to the Department of Public Health's rules entitled Asbestos Abatement for Public and Private Schools and Commercial and Public Buildings (77 Ill Adm Code 855; 22 Ill Reg 4632) because these rules place an undue economic burden on those regulated, especially small business flooring contractors and retailers and building owners. The requirements of these rules for floor tile removal would substantially raise the costs associated with this activity, which may not be commensurate with the hazard raised.

Normally, failure of the agency to respond within 90 days after receipt of the Statement of Objection would constitute withdrawal of this proposed rulemaking. In this case, since the one year limitation on this rulemaking is reached on 3/13/99, the regular 90 day period is shortened. The agency's response will be placed on the JCAR agenda for further consideration.

ILLINOIS REGISTER 2823
99

JOINT COMMITTEE ON ADMINISTRATIVE RULES

ILLINOIS GENERAL ASSEMBLY

SECOND NOTICES RECEIVED

The following second notice was received by the Joint Committee on Administrative Rules during the period of February 17, 1999 through February 22, 1999 and has been scheduled for review by the Committee at its March 16, 1999 meetings in Springfield. Other items not contained in this published list may also be considered. Members of the public wishing to express their views with respect to a rule should submit written comments to the Committee at the following address: Joint Committee on Administrative Rules, 700 Stratton Bldg., Springfield IL 62706.

Second Notice Expires	Agency and Rule	Start Of First Notice	JCAR Meeting
4/2/99	Secretary of State, Lobbyist Registration and Reports (2 Ill Adm Code 560)	12/28/98 22 Ill Reg 22218	3/16/99
4/7/99	Secretary of State, The Illinois State Library Training Program Grants (23 Ill Adm Code 3070)	12/4/98 22 Ill Reg 20806	3/16/99
4/7/99	State Board of Elections, Approval of Voting Systems (26 Ill Adm Code 204)	5/8/98 22 Ill Reg 7853	3/16/98
4/7/99	State Board of Elections, Registration of Voters (26 Ill Adm Code 216)	5/8/98 22 Ill Reg 7866	3/16/99

Vol. 23, Issue 10   ISSUES INDEX   March 5, 1999

Rules acted upon during the calender quarter from Issue 1 through Issue 16 are listed in the Issues Index by Title number, Part number and Issue number. For example, 50 Ill. Adm. Code 2500 published in Issue 1 will be listed as 50-2500-1. The letter "R" designates a rule that is being repealed. Inquiries about the Issues Index may be directed to the Administrative Code Division at 217-782-4414 or jmatale@iccgate.sos.state.il.us (Internet address).

PROPOSED			
2-1076-10	89-684-1	82-120-6	80-2700-2
2-3000-6	89-686-1	68-590-2	89-112-2,4
2-3001-6		68-610-2	89-113-2
2-3002-6	**ADOPTED**	68-1250-6	89-114-2
8-600-2	8-20-2	68-1315-6	89-121-7
17-670-4	8-40-2	77-245-4	
23-25-7	8-55-2	77-250-4	**PEREMPTORY**
23-260-6	8-75-2	77-300-4	80-310-3
23-1501-1	8-80-2	77-330-4	
23-2700-6	8-85-2	77-340-4	
23-2720-6	8-100-2	77-350-4	
23-2761-6	8-105-2	77-370-4	
23-2733-6	8-110-2	77-390-4	
23-2735-6	8-115-2	77-2200-6	
23-2737-6	8-125-2	80-310-3	
23-2771-6	17-3045	83-415-5	
23-2790-6	23-1038-10	83-505-5	
26-100-3	23-2775-7	83-745-6	
26-125-4	23-3040-6,7	89-104-6	
32-331-5	32-401-1	89-112-4,6	
35-307-3	32-410-1	89-113-6	
35 807-7	35-106-9	89-114-6	
35-808-1	35-304-1	89-118-2	
35-809-1,7	35-611-10	89-120-6	
35-811-1	35-703-6	89-125-2	
44-1-10	35-720-6	89-144-4	
56-2665-4	35-721-6	89-160-6	
68-1175-6	35-724-6	89-240-7	
68-1320-1	35-725-6	89-315-7	
77-830-5	35-728-6	89-316-7	
77-2060-5	35-738-6	89-431-3	
80-2700-2	35-739-6	89-553-5	
83-451-1,5	35-741-2	89-563-5	
89-10-7	35-811-10	89-567-5	
89-112-2,4	41-120-1	89-572-6	
89-113-1,2	44-1120-4	89-590-1	
89-114-2	47-310-5	89-617-5	
89-121-7	50-2500-1	89-679-6	
89-140-1	50-2505-1	92-554-3	
89-148-4	50-2510-1	92-1001-3	
89-360-4	50-2515-1		
89-402-7	50-2520-1	**EMERGENCY**	
89-593-5	50-2525-1	17-670-10	
89-676-1	50-2770-1	26-100-3	
89-679-5	59-135-6	26-125-4	
	59-119-1	44-1-10	

CPSIA information can be obtained
at www.ICGtesting.com
Printed in the USA
BVHW060925041218
534639BV00018BA/884/P